I Remember
PAYNE STEWART

I Remember
PAYNE STEWART

*Personal Memories of Golf's Most Dapper Champion
by the People Who Knew Him Best*

MICHAEL ARKUSH

Cumberland House
Nashville, Tennessee

Published by Cumberland House Publishing, Inc., 431 Harding Industrial Drive, Nashville, Tennessee 37211

Jacket design by Bruce Gore
Cover photo provided by AP/Wide World Photos
Text design by Bruce Gore, Gore Studios, Inc.

Library of Congress Cataloging-in-Publication Data

Arkush, Michael.
    I remember Payne Stewart : personal memories of golf's most dapper champion by the people who knew him best / Michael Arkush.
        p. cm.
    Includes index.
    ISBN 1-58182-082-8 (alk. paper)
    1. Stewart, Payne, 1957–1999--Anecdotes. 2. Stewart, Payne, 1957–1999--Friends and associates. 3. Golfers--United States--Biography. I. Title.

    GV964.S84 A75 2000
    796.352'092--dc21
    [B]

                                                        00-022686

Printed in the United States of America
3 4 5 6 7 8 9 — 04 03 02 01 00

To Pauletta

CONTENTS

ACKNOWLEDGMENTS

As usual, there are numerous people to thank for contributing to this project. For starters, I owe a tremendous debt to those who agreed to be interviewed. They were very generous with their time and spoke quite candidly. They are: Peter Alliss, Dave Anderson, Larry Atwood, Todd Awe, Andy Bean, Chip Beck, Guy Boros, Don Brauer, Mark Brooks, Reagan Brown, Brad Bryant, Paul Celano, Jim Colbert, J. B. Collingsworth, Bob Condron, Ben Crenshaw, Nathaniel Crosby, Jayne Custred, Burt Darden, Jay Delsing, Brian DePasquale, Bruce Devlin, Jaime Diaz, Brad Faxon, David Feherty, John Feinstein, Bruce Fleisher, Eric Fredricksen, Shawn Freeman, Jim Gallagher Jr., John Gentry, Chuck Gerber, John Goldstein,

David Graham, Joe Greene, Melanie Hauser, Jim Henry, Bruce Hollowell, Jim Holtgrieve, Joe Inman, Tony Jacklin, Randall James, Terry Jastrow, Drue Johnson, Mitch Kemper, Peter Kessler, Peter Kostis, Bill Kratzert, Perry Leslie, Bruce Lietzke, Mike Lupica, Mark Lye, Bill Macatee, Andrew Magee, Roger Maltbie, Carol Mann, Tom Martin, Gary McCord, Mark McCumber, Tom Meeks, Steve Melnyk, Johnny Miller, Larry Moody, Jim Morris, Paul Mullins, Jim Nantz, Byron Nelson, Andy North, Kyle O'Brien-Stevens, Christy O'Connor Jr., David Ogrin, Tom O'Toole Jr., Jerry Pate, Mike Peck, Calvin Peete, Kenny Perry, Gary Player, Cathy Reynolds, Sam Reynolds, Larry Rinker, Jimmy Roberts, Chi Chi Rodriguez, Mark Rolfing, Tommy Roy, Charlie Rymer, Doug Sanders, Scott Simpson, Craig Smith, Dave Stockton, Greg Stoda, Steve Szurlej, Lora Thomas, Donna Thompson, Mike Tirico, Lee Trevino, Scott Van Pelt, Bob Verdi, Brendan Walsh, E. Harvie Ward, Jack Whitaker, Mark Wiebe, Chuck Will, Keith Williams, and Guy Yocom. I am especially grateful to Payne Stewart's mother, Bee, who spoke lovingly about her son for nearly an hour, and to Payne's sister, Susan Daniel, for providing some wonderful photos.

At *Golf World*, I must thank Jerry Tarde, Terry Galvin, and Geoff Russell for their support. I'm grateful, as well, to my colleague and friend, Bill Fields, whose expertise in the game cannot be overestimated. Jim Oberman, Howard Richman, and Mark Langill were also extremely helpful. I don't know how I would have managed without their invaluable assistance.

Once again, as was the case with my four previous books, my wife, Pauletta, deserves the greatest praise. Her spirit and sensitivity inspired me throughout the whole process. I would also like to thank my daughter, Jade, who has such a promising future in whatever she chooses to do with her life. Her boundless energy is a constant motivation. Now if I could only convince her to try golf.

I owe a special debt to my agent, Jay Mandel, my editor, Mike Towle, and my aunt and uncle, Ann and Abe Ainspan, who introduced me to a game that has remained my passion ever since.

INTRODUCTION

IN THE FIRST FEW hours after Payne Stewart was killed last October, I couldn't afford to feel a thing. There wasn't time. The crash happened in the middle of our weekly Monday deadline at *Golf World*, forcing us to frantically compile the details of the accident, as well as to coordinate the reaction from his devastated friends and contemporaries throughout the golf community. Finally, shortly before 10:00 P.M., I drove home, proud of the package we put together for our readers.

Then it hit me. It hit me hard. I thought back to the sunny afternoon in the summer of 1997 when I approached Payne to do an interview for my book (*Fairways and Dreams*) about professional golfers and the fathers who inspired them. Frankly, I had been a bit apprehensive, fearful the encounter might go as poorly as the first time I talked to him in early 1996 on the putting green at Torrey Pines Golf Club in California. That time, he had been sarcastic and dismissive. Payne could be that way, other golf writers later told me. I braced myself for the possibility he might be that way again.

He wasn't. In fact, he could not have been more gracious. Then, once we later did the interview, he was articulate and emotional, reflecting on the valuable lessons he had learned from his late father, traveling salesman Bill Stewart. He never, not for a second, exhibited the kind of impatience PGA Tour players frequently show when they would rather be beating balls on the driving range or hanging out with their buddies in the locker room. We didn't have an interview; we had a conversation.

"That man, wiser than I ever realized," said Payne, referring to his father, "taught me how to compete and how to care passionately about whatever you're doing, which, in my profession, is absolutely essential."

Soon, as I continued to drive home, the memory of that wonderful afternoon faded. I was back in the present, a present I suddenly wanted to avoid. What puzzled me the most, however, on that October night, and in the ensuing days, was why I had become so distraught about Payne's death in the first place. It wasn't as if I had been particularly close to the guy; I wasn't. Countless other golf writers knew him much better. Yet I couldn't help but feel that I had suffered a big loss, which didn't make any sense.

Then, once I started working on this book, it made perfect sense. In my own way, I could relate to the courageous effort Payne had undergone to make himself a better person, and I'm far from alone. Many of us try every day to reach our full potential. We try to improve as husbands and wives, as fathers and mothers, as sons and daughters. We don't always succeed, of course, which is why when we see someone who does make big strides, it touches our souls in ways we may never fully understand. It gives us hope in our own challenges, and makes us feel more connected to each other.

This book attempts to chronicle Payne's journey of self-discovery. Unlike a more conventional approach, it doesn't pretend to delve into every aspect of his life or to be the definitive Payne Stewart biography. Instead, in conversations with about one hundred friends and contemporaries, it unveils Payne in a montage of snapshots often out of the public eye. In their unfiltered honesty, they unmask the spirit and soul of a passionate hero from the heartland who, in both life and death, found a special place in America's hearts.

—*Michael Arkush*

I Remember
PAYNE STEWART

SPRINGFIELD

He took his U.S. Open trophy out there, and everybody had the chance to have their picture taken with it. This was his hometown. That's what he told them.

—BEE PAYNE-STEWART, HIS MOM

Payne Stewart always appreciated a good duel on the golf course, making it most fitting that he grew up in Springfield, Missouri, which had been well acquainted with duels long before its citizens ever heard of this strange game. In July 1865, only a few months after the Civil War ended, the town square became the site of the nation's first recorded shoot-out. The combatants were: "Wild Bill" Hickok and Dave Tutt. As the story goes, Tutt, claiming that Hickok owed him money from a poker game, seized his pocket watch as collateral. He then said he would wear it in public as a sign that Hickok hadn't paid up. It was apparently decided that a duel was the only way to settle the matter. Tutt fired the first shot, and missed; Hickok fired the next, and didn't.[1]

Springfield also carries the distinction of being the city where, on April 30, 1926, officials proposed the name of the new Chicago-to-Los Angeles highway—the soon-to-be famous Route 66. Stretching from the Great Lakes to the Pacific Coast, it became, in 1938, the first completely paved transcontinental highway in America.[2] Almost forty years later, the eighteen-year-old Payne, like so many in his generation, hit the road, in his case bound for a new life at Southern Methodist University in Dallas. Yet whatever lessons he was to pick up at college or on the PGA Tour, none would ever be as profound as the ones he learned at home.

Born January 30, 1957, William Payne Stewart was the third child, and first son, of Bill and Bee Stewart. From the beginning, Bill Stewart, a well-traveled salesman and outstanding amateur golfer, took a deep interest in this youngster. The two spent countless hours at Hickory Hills Country Club, where Payne was introduced to the game that would someday become his livelihood. He also developed numerous friendships with people in Springfield, who, to this day, maintain a certain proprietorship over their hometown hero. You can't blame them. They are the ones who watched him evolve from a boy into a man into a father and, eventually, into a champion.

———

Even as a kid, Payne was ready with the well-timed retort, a skill he would employ constantly over the years. It would also, however, became a skill that, on many occasions, would get him into loads of trouble with the press and even his pals. He simply didn't pause often enough to consider the possible repercussions. **Bee Payne-Stewart** *traces the origin of her son's quick wit:*

Since he was the youngest one in the neighborhood, he was always following everybody around, wanting to do

Even as a youngster, Payne sometimes had that certain look that some kind of mischief might be right around the corner. (Photo courtesy of Susan Daniel)

what they were doing. So, of course, with his being the youngest one, the boys in the neighborhood teased him. That's how he learned to be such a jokester. Because he had to come back to all these older fellows, he was always pretty sharp in what he had to say to them. His older sisters went after these kids to stop teasing him. His sisters loved him dearly, although he did like to tattle on them if he could find out something about them.

———

*As the assistant club professional at Hickory Hills in the 1970s, **Perry Leslie** spent a lot of time around Payne during his adolescence. Looking back more than twenty years later, Leslie reflects on a youngster who displayed plenty of pure ability, even if his level of dedication wasn't always something to emulate:*

From the time Payne was five years old, he was going to be nothing but a PGA Tour player. He never considered doing anything else. You always knew he was going to be a good player, but because we had so many other good players around the club at that time, there was really no reason to suspect that he was going to end up being, well, Payne Stewart. Plus he had some real good competition as a kid. In fact, there were a few people at Hickory who could beat him, and, besides, he had no real terrific work ethic. During our organized junior lessons, he would hit a couple of balls perfectly and then go over to the swimming pool to chase girls. Then he would come back and do it all over again. This went on for quite some time. As a matter of fact, he probably hit fewer balls than half the kids out there did. But I guess that's because he didn't have to. If there was ever anyone born with it, it was Payne. My brother organized a series of junior tournaments for the kids and ran them all summer long in Jefferson City. At that time, there was really no place in Springfield for kids to play junior golf. Payne played in those tournaments for several years and won just about everything.

All the money games generally took place at the municipal golf course, but Bill Stewart established a few at the country club and got Payne involved in them at a pretty young age. He was probably fourteen or fifteen. He taught Payne to put it on the line and to play for it, which, obviously, would become pretty important in his profession. Bill didn't do it for the big money but merely to teach him that aspect of the game, that you had to be fiercely competitive in order to be successful. Payne learned that lesson very well. Bill was a great model for Payne. He was the perfect gamer. He looked like he'd shoot about 100, hitting these horrible duck-hook drives, but he was the kind of guy who would be four down in a match with three to go and still be trying to figure out a way to beat you.

Payne and his father were a real special twosome. They had an unbelievable relationship. They would hug and even kiss each other on the lips in public. You didn't see many fathers and sons doing that. You still don't. His dad was a very colorful character. Bill, all the time, dressed like Payne later did on the tour. He wore these loud, plaid coats and ties that didn't match, and he had a famous sweater that was actually framed after his death and put in the men's locker room at Hickory Hills. They nicknamed it "Bill's blankey," and it's kind of a tradition at the club that, for good luck, you touch that picture as you go out to play. It started out bright orange and by the time he got through wearing it about forty years later, it had a big brown spot on the right shoulder where he used to carry his bags.

Although he was not a formal instructor at the club, Bill Stewart, a two-time Missouri Amateur champion (1953 and 1957) knew how critical a good short game would be in his son's future. Which is why, as family friend **Donna Thompson** *points out, he didn't waste any time showing Payne the value of the recovery shot. They even developed a routine:*

It would be getting close to dark at the club and Bill would say, "Buss"—he called him Buss—"you make this in two and you can call it a day." And then he'd throw the ball in all these weird places. That's why Payne, whenever he made a bad drive over the years and had to make a great shot to save his par, had the ability to do it. That's because Bill had always made him practice that shot more than anything else. They would spend a lot of time together at the club. Even when it was chilly, if the range was open, they were out there hitting balls pretty much daily when Bill was in town.

Golf's most sharp-dressed man was dashing and debonair at an early age. (Photo courtesy of Susan Daniel)

Payne didn't necessarily need a driving range to work on his game. He could get a lot accomplished inside the Stewart home with the help, according to older sister, **Lora Thomas***, of some overmatched friends:*

When he was in grade school, he would have friends over to spend the night and his favorite thing to do was to have a putting contest. That's the *last* thing a couple of these guys wanted to do because Payne made the rules and he had the game down. We had this metal thing that you could stand up real tall or make real flat. You'd putt into that and then the ball would come right back to you. It had a hole in the middle that was painted green. Back then, we didn't have Blockbuster Video or Nintendo, so you had to invent other things to do at home. Of course, Payne would win all the time. I would say, "Hal doesn't want to play that, he knows you're going to win." He'd say it was his friend and they would do whatever they wanted.

———◦◦◦———

The work at the club—and on the carpet—paid off. Payne gradually got better and better. He became so accomplished that when he was about fourteen years old, he broke 70 for the first time. **Joe Greene**, *a frequent member of Bill Stewart's foursome, recalls the significance of that occasion, although it was clearly the teacher, not the pupil, who seemed more excited:*

His dad was in tears while Payne was pretty blasé about it. He always had the confidence that he could do just about anything he wanted to do and he was often right. That day, his dad, who didn't drink, told me he almost took a drink in celebration of his son's achievement. Bill was such a supporter. The high school athletic association would not allow parents to accompany children during any competition. I think it's because it was felt they would interfere too much with their kids' play. It's still a rule today. So Bill would get in a car and drive very slowly around the perimeter of the golf course to watch Payne play. I'm not saying he saw every single shot, but he certainly saw more than he would have if he had stayed home.

Payne, to be sure, was very much into gamesmanship, just like his dad. In the middle of a match, he would say things like, "How's your grip?" or "Your grip looks different today" or "Isn't your stance wider than it used to be?" These were lines that were designed to make you think about things you shouldn't be thinking about while you're playing golf, and they often worked. I don't think

11

he ever played a match that he wasn't seriously interested in winning. There was no such thing as a casual round.

━━◁◦▷━━

Payne's competitiveness was not confined to his own matches. As good friend **Bruce Hollowell** *explains, Payne could be just as intense when carrying someone else's clubs, such as the time he accompanied his father to the Western Amateur in Rockford, Illinois. So what if it was only a practice round? As far as Payne was concerned, it might as well have been the final round of the U.S. Open:*

Payne was only fourteen or fifteen and getting to be a pretty good player but not good enough yet to play in the tournament. So instead, he caddied for his dad, who was playing with me and Jim Morris, probably Bill's closest friend. Yet the passion and fire he showed as a caddie was simply incredible. Jim and Bill, as was often the case, played for a few shekels. Still, since this was a practice round, there was really no reason to expect too much excitement. You were there, basically, to get to know the course and to be ready when the competition got under way for keeps. But for the whole time that day, Payne was on Jim's butt, saying things like, "Hook it. Shank it. Knock it into the water." He even yelled on Jim's backswing. Though he couldn't play that day, he wanted his dad so badly to win. That's the kind of competitiveness that Payne always displayed. Always.

His father was on him all the time: "Watch this. Here's how I do this. Here's how I do that." There was so much camaraderie between the two of them. Yet at the same time, his father would do everything he could to beat his son, teaching him all kinds of things along the way. Bill wouldn't let down for a second. He was such a practitioner around the greens. Bill worked more on Payne's short game than on anything else. He figured that Payne already had such a natural golf swing that there was no reason to mess with it. He worked with him all the time on the thirty-yard and forty-yard shot—a shot that, as most people know, became huge in Payne's career. Then, after Bill was done teaching Payne everything he could, he handed him over to Sam Reynolds, our local pro who did a great job with him.

—◄◄∭◐∭►—

Sam Reynolds, by all accounts, did do a great job with his young student, once he was able to pry him away from an extremely cautious Bill Stewart:

Bill was very, very protective of Payne, but he knew that he was limited in his golf knowledge. He was a very good player but he didn't know as much as I did. As Payne got to be about fifteen, Bill said to me, "Okay, Sam, I'm going to let you work with him for two hours. In two hours, I'm coming back." Payne and I would then hit balls and talk for two hours. We would work on balance, footwork, and the proper takeaway. Then, in exactly two hours, Bill would come back in his cart and that would be it for the day. This went on right up through the end of high school.

My teacher, Leland "Duke" Gibson [head pro at Blue Hills Country Club in Kansas City] taught me how to play with good rhythm and balance on your feet, and that's what I always taught. All rhythm is created from your feet, then you let the upper part of your body blend with the rhythm of your feet. I wasn't necessarily focused on Payne;

he was one of a bunch of kids. He just took it to a different level because of the inspiration he got from his father. Payne was very careful about taking advice from anybody in those days except his father and me. He was generally not very trusting; his father instilled that into him: "Don't listen to anybody unless I tell you." It was a great honor for Bill to allow me to work with his son. I didn't work with Payne every day and yet I did. Let me explain. It was all about being exposed to a picture of the golf swing being done properly. He would watch me hit hundreds of balls a day. Payne, like many kids, learned by mimicking. It wasn't an official lesson, and yet it served the same purpose.

Jim Morris didn't allow Payne's antics to get in the way of their friendship. The two eventually hooked up as teammates for the annual pro-am tournament at Pebble Beach. Morris, sixty-nine, can still pinpoint the moment in the early 1970s when he realized that this brash youngster had a chance to become a special player. It happened, as one might imagine, in the middle of competition:

I was playing Payne, who was sixteen, in the finals of the club championship. Meanwhile, as usual, Bill was circling the golf course. He finally came into the pro shop when I had Payne three or four down after twenty-seven holes of a thirty-six-hole match and took him over into the corner. I could tell that he was getting on him pretty hard. Well, whatever he said, it sure worked. Because Payne went out on the back side and shot four or five under. Yes, I was lucky to squeak by and win the championship, but the way Payne played convinced me he had the right stuff. He was probably hitting it about

270 off the tee, but could move the ball 300 yards any time he wanted to.

Payne had great genes. I remember when his dad, back in the days when neither one of us could put a couple of nickels together, was playing against one of the best players in the state, a young man by the name of Jim Tom Blair, who was the son of the governor. Jim was a beautiful ball striker. It was a thirty-six-hole final at Hickory Hills, and Bill was the underdog. I bet a good deal of money on him, probably way more than I had in my pocket. Anyway, with two holes to go, Bill was two down and I go up to him at seventeen and say, "Billy, you've given him a heck of a match," and he says to me, in all honesty, in those steely eyes of his: "Brother, I've got him." So you know what he does? He wins the next two holes to tie him, making twenty-footers each time, and then knocks in a forty-footer on the third play-off hole to win. So you see how competitive Bill Stewart was in his own right. He just didn't have the ability to hit it far enough, and he had to work for a living. It was a different era in those days. There wasn't big money available for a professional golfer. Bill also had a knack for getting you to believe that you might do something great. He certainly got Payne to believe that.

—————

For all his power and intensity, Payne was far from invincible. Springfield did breed some pretty good players in the 1970s, including **John Gentry**. *Gentry, however, who currently chairs the golf committee at Hickory Hills, couldn't match his friend's advantages:*

He played quite frequently with his father and his father's friends while the rest of us were out playing among ourselves. We were involved in junior golf being taught by the pro staff, which basically was three or four pros giving lessons and a whole bunch of kids lining up every Friday morning during the summer. Payne, at a fairly young age, stopped participating in that group because he was receiving direction from his father. I wouldn't say we were jealous, but you could certainly see the benefits that it provided him. He was able to pick up a whole different perspective on the game that either some of us never got or didn't get until we were much older. Playing with or against people older than you can enhance your game in a major way. You become more immune to pressure the more you're exposed to it. He was exposed to the pressure of having to play above his best because he was playing with good players.

Bill Stewart is often credited for Payne's growth as a golfer and, perhaps more importantly, as a person. But it would be a big mistake to neglect the contributions that **Bee Payne-Stewart** *made to her son's upbringing. Bee, who still resides in Springfield, states her case:*

One thing that everybody has always written about is how close he was to his father, but his father was gone during the week. I was the one who took him to the golf course to practice. I was the one who always disciplined him. His father wasn't around to do it and, besides, his father wouldn't have done it anyway. But that's the way it is with women who are home all the time. They get little credit. Bill traveled three states and sold bed springs. He was one of their top salesmen, which meant he had to pay a lot of attention to his customers. When he'd leave Monday mornings, he'd leave behind instructions for all of us—"Now, Bee, you make him practice. You make the girls do this." There were always instructions about what I had to do, and then I just did what I wanted to do. He said he'd be home Friday. Usually, he would come in on Thursday nights. So we'd hurry up and get everything done before he arrived. He was a good father, very bossy, but he wasn't cruel.

———

*Payne attended Greenwood Laboratory School, a small private facility on the grounds of Southwest Missouri State University in the center of Springfield. There were only thirty students in his class, including his good friend, **Keith Williams**, who later became a physician in town. As Williams sees it, Payne belonged to a rather harmless group of teenage boys:*

We did everything that kids do at that age. Let me be very clear, though. We never got into any trouble. I'm talking about small things, like skipping school. It's not like we were real ambitious. We'd usually wind up at McDonald's or somewhere else getting a bite to eat. Payne had an uncanny sense of knowing when a prank could be pulled off and when it couldn't be pulled off. That was pretty mature for someone his age. I remember the time that he and I and another friend took his mom's blue convertible out to the drive-in when it was about zero degrees out. We decided we were going to put the top down. It seemed like a funny idea. It wasn't. The windows cracked open. His parents were not pleased.

Payne and I used to double-date a lot, going to movies and other functions around town. Once we even took our dates quail hunting. They just kind of trailed along; I don't think they had the best time. A lot of times, we'd sneak into the drive-in theaters with our dates and be in the back smooching. That's all you did in those days. If we had tried to do more, we would have been in big trouble.

He had a million friends in high school. If you wanted to do everything, Greenwood was the kind of place that gave you that experience. He didn't play big-time football until his junior year, when he became the starting quarterback. In basketball, he had a good sophomore year. So good, in fact, that expectations were pretty high for his junior year, although he floundered a bit. Everyone was kind of down on him, although it wasn't like he had been college material before that. After all, you had to be a megastar at Greenwood to even be looked at by any colleges.

There was a bias against him in the classroom. The teachers had a feeling that he was a B or C student when, in fact, he was better than that. I remember a number of times that we would go over things for hours and hours. He would know the material and yet he would still end up with B's and C's on tests and essays. We had one class where we decided we were going to try to prove our theory. So several of us who were making A's at the time actually wrote the papers for him, and he turned them in. Well, we made A's, while he made B's and C's. Meanwhile, Payne's girlfriend, who attended a different school, wrote an essay. When the same subject came up at Greenwood, Payne took her essay and just retyped it, knowing that his teacher would have no idea that it had been plagiarized. Anyway, he ended up with a C on it while she had gotten an A.

We never went to the administrators about it. After all, Payne knew by his sophomore or junior year that his means to an end depended on his ability in golf, not his academic abilities. Even though he wasn't saying that he was going to be a professional golfer, he darn well knew that if he were going to go to SMU, it would be on a golf scholarship. My theory, and it's only a theory, was that the bias occurred because Payne's sister, who had gone to the same school, had not been the greatest student in the world. The way the teachers looked at it, how could Payne really be any different?

—————

*For all his academic difficulties, Payne managed to buckle down in school when he had a good reason. Like many mothers who became experts at child psychology, **Bee Payne-Stewart** knew how to find one:*

When he was sixteen, boy, he wanted that driver's license. I took him down to the motor vehicle department, and he was top-notch, A-1 on that driver's test. I said, "Honey, isn't that great? You've got the knowledge there. Now if you want to start driving, you have to make the honor roll [a minimum B average]." So he started making the Honor Roll and I let him drive the car. We couldn't buy him a car, so he used ours, a white and blue Gremlin. It was a darling little car. He was a smart kid who just didn't apply himself. He always had the where-withal to do it.

—————

A lot of Payne's golfing prowess was passed on to him by his father, Bill Stewart, shown here holding the trophy symbolic of his winning the Missouri state amateur golf championship in 1953. (Photo courtesy of Susan Daniel)

Payne also had the wherewithal to make some pretty bold decisions, such as the time when, at the age of seventeen, he sent away for an engagement ring that he planned to give to his sweetheart. Not surprisingly, his father, as **Bee Payne-Stewart** *remembers, wasn't too thrilled:*

Since Payne had ordered it from a friend of ours who sold jewelry in California, it came right to our house, which is how I happened to open it and show it to his dad. It wasn't addressed to Payne. We asked him about it and told him that we were going to have to send it back. Bill said, "Listen, guy, you're not ready for marriage yet. You're going to get a college education." That was always our goal with all of our kids. Payne wasn't belligerent about it in the least. He didn't have much to say, really. I know he certainly didn't have the money to pay for a ring.

———

The exchange over the ring wasn't the only time during his adolescence that Payne clashed with his more conventional father. **Bee Payne-Stewart** *cites another occasion, although this time, she took her son's side:*

When he was in high school, he decided he wanted to grow sideburns. Well, all the hippies were growing sideburns back then. This was in the early 1970s, when this kind of stuff was still going on. I thought that the sideburns were okay, but when his father saw them, he took that little kid into the bathroom to shave them off right away. It was so cruel. I was so mad I cried. It just broke my heart, and I know it broke Payne's heart because he came out of the bathroom crying. When he was in college, I encouraged him to get a perm, which he did. His dad didn't like that, either. Bill was very conservative.

—◦—

Payne fit in quite well at Greenwood. Nowhere was that more evident, perhaps, than in his participation in sports. As classmate **Tom Martin** *points out, Payne was very determined:*

He had one game as a junior where he threw more interceptions than completions. All of us, of course, gave him a hard time, including his dad. But, like with everything else, Payne worked at it and got better, and he had a pretty good senior year. I think he ended up second-team all-conference, which was a big achievement. I don't recall his pulling out a particular game at the end, but I do remember his throwing a few long touchdown passes to our tight end. In basketball, we had a good team. We won the conference and lost in the quarterfinals of the state. The basketball coach used to ride him harder than anyone else on the team. I guess that was because Payne, who played guard, was a pretty good player and the coach felt like he could be even better.

—◦—

As much effort as Payne put forth into being a good quarterback, football coach **Paul Mullins** *recalls more about his exploits off the field:*

He was a jokester in the locker room. He would put these red-hot bombs, which were used to loosen up muscles, in other guys' jockstraps. He would also wrap tape around people's combination locks so that they would have a

Payne excelled at sports, including golf, in high school before graduating and going on to join the golf team at Southern Methodist University in Dallas. (Photo courtesy of Susan Daniel)

hard time getting into them. If anybody was checking into some mischief that had been done around the school, the standing joke would be: "Well, all I know is that Payne Stewart might have done it." A lot of times, of course, he hadn't done it, but that was still the joke.

———

*Last July (1999), with regards to Payne, there were no more stand-ing jokes in Springfield—only standing fans. The hometown hero, fresh from capturing his second U.S. Open title, was back for a visit. At the local municipal course renamed for him and his father, he was treated to a special welcome that many, such as **John Gentry**, will always cherish:*

We had a reception line that seemed to go on forever. When it was finally our time, we had a real good chat. I guess Payne had a good memory because he reminisced about the early days, telling my boys about when he and I were kids and how good a golfer I used to be. They enjoyed hearing that, and, so, of course, did I, although I think he embellished things just a bit. Anyway, the point is that he wasn't standing up there with a big chest and shoulders thrown back, boasting about all his great accomplishments. He was very human. Instead of talking about himself, he was talking about others. It wasn't the classic story of the Hollywood star forgetting everybody in his hometown.

—⊶⊶—

Nobody, to be sure, felt more pride during the homecoming than **Bee Payne-Stewart**:

They had one of these movable stages with microphones set up on the course. The family got up there but not Payne. He went right into the pro shop and talked to people in there, and when it was time for the program to start, he went straight to where they were going to have him hit balls. He didn't make any kind of a speech; he wasn't having any of that formal stuff. He took his U.S. Open trophy out there, and everybody had the chance to have their picture taken with it. This was his hometown. That's what he told them, "I might live in Orlando, but my home is in Springfield."

—⊶⊶—

*Later that evening, after the reception and another gathering at Hickory Hills had finally ended, Payne and a few friends went to a bar in town to cap off the wonderful day. **Bruce Hollowell** was part of the group who probably didn't want the evening to ever end:*

We all sat around, had a beer and just talked. Payne was so unbelievably happy with his life. You could see it in the way he carried on a simple conversation. And everybody was so happy for him. At one point, he went outside and brought back the U.S. Open trophy he had won at Pinehurst. He then proceeded to talk to the owner who came back with a couple of bottles of champagne, which were passed around the table. Of the five couples there, everybody took a small sip except me. I let it pass by me twice. I drink beer, not champagne. But Payne looked over and could tell what I was doing. He said, "By golly, it's so hard to win the U.S. Open, I may never win one again. You better take a drink." So I did. I took probably five or six sips. I'll never forget that.

THE COLLEGE YEARS

When I first saw him play that week, there was sort of a cross between a wonderful grace and style with his swing combined with a little swagger, even as an amateur. It was really nice to see.

—STEVE MELNYK,
TV GOLF COMMENTATOR

In 1975 Payne left Greenwood for a new life at Southern Methodist University (SMU), in Dallas. While the school didn't rank among the elite programs in college golf, it would, eventually, offer Payne an opportunity to challenge himself on a regular basis in the highly regarded Southwest Conference against prominent players such as Blaine McCallister [University of Houston], David Ogrin [Texas A&M], Phil Blackmar [University of Texas], and, of course, Fred Couples [University of Houston]. It would be the first of many challenges in his career, one that might determine whether he had enough ability and desire to reach his ultimate goal—the PGA Tour.

SMU, like so many other campuses, served as a sanctuary, promising a final fling with freedom before the demands and responsibilities of the real world would take over. Four years would go by fast, too fast, so students made sure to sneak in as much fun as possible—at bars, fraternities, football games, anywhere—when they weren't hitting the books.

———

Payne, however, might have had too much fun. Fortunately, it didn't take long, says **Perry Leslie***, before word of Payne's misguided priorities made its way back to Springfield and, more importantly, to the Stewart household:*

He almost went sideways there, almost really blowing it by letting his golf game and his studies become second to his partying. It happens to a lot of people at that stage of life, but his dad was a strong enough personality that when he found out what was going on, he sat Payne down one day, pointed a finger at his nose, and he said, "If you think that you're going to play professional golf, son, you're not getting another penny unless you get straightened out. You can just forget about your professional career because it isn't going to happen."

———

Bee Payne-Stewart, *though, offers another interpretation:*

I was the one who saw that he was not doing well and I was the one who made him go to summer school at SMU. Not his father, who, again, wasn't around as much because he was on the road most of the week. I don't know which exact year it was, but one of the faculty members at SMU had some relatives who lived in a small town close to Springfield, and they told me that Payne wasn't doing too well. The same faculty member then wrote to me because she was his adviser. Well, eventually, he did buckle down and make his grades. He majored in business just in case the golf thing didn't work out.

—⊸◆⊷—

*The golf thing, of course, did work out, although the image of Payne at SMU was, according to teammate **Reagan Brown**, much different than the one he would try to cultivate years later on the PGA Tour:*

People viewed him in his appearances at the Ryder Cup as a real leader and a big cheerleader, and rightfully so. But he was not like that at all in college. He was a lot more reticent and into working on his own game. He was not a cheerleader at all. He was not critical of other people. Most of the time, he was not your hit-balls-until-your-hands-bleed type of person. He liked to play more than he liked to practice, which is no criticism. I think that Payne started working at his game a lot harder beginning in his junior year and certainly by his senior year. He may have practiced a lot during the summer, but at school he spent more time having fun than anything else. Yet with a swing like his, all the players on the team kidded him, "Why do you need to practice?" His swing was so effortless, and one that was easy to repeat without any significant flaws. And he was such a tremendous wedge player around the greens.

—⊸◆⊷—

In 1978 Payne finally began to fulfill his potential. Soon, he became one of the best players in the highly competitive Southwest Conference, perhaps even in the nation. The PGA Tour seemed like a real possibility. He also spent more time on his studies.
Reagan Brown *noticed the new commitment:*

Payne was probably a mediocre student his first couple of years, not because he wasn't smart, but because he just didn't apply himself. But I did see that by his senior year, he had cut out a lot of the kidding and seemed to be a little more devoted to schoolwork. He obviously stepped it up a lot between his junior and senior years to be able to graduate with some decent grades. He deserves credit for that. After all, in the 1970s there were a lot of people who went to school to play golf, and that's all they were there for. They couldn't care less about how they did in classes. But one of the things I was most proud of about Payne was that he got his degree in four years and did pretty well. That was a real mark of achievement for him and for the way he was raised by his parents.

As for golf, while I was going to law school at the University of Texas, Payne was still a senior at SMU. So when the team came to play a match in Austin [the Morris Williams Intercollegiate], I went down to see them play. I walked the last nine holes. I might have even carried Payne's bag. The thing I noticed more than anything else was that he seemed a lot more focused on what he was doing, showing the kind of intensity everyone would see years later when he was coming down the stretch of the U.S. Open. That was the first time I had ever seen it, and it made me think that this guy had a shot to make it as a pro. He obviously had the game, and now he also had the killer instinct to close the deal. It was suddenly, "I am going to do well," as opposed to, "I've got a good game and a good swing and whatever happens, happens."

Before, he would tend to lose concentration. He would hit a bad shot and not concentrate anymore. He wouldn't focus on the next thing because he couldn't get over the fact that something was going wrong. But on that day in Austin, that wasn't happening anymore. There also wasn't a lot of the joking around that he had done. In the last year of college, much of what coach Earl Stewart [no relation] said started to have benefits in helping Payne understand that all the physical talent in the world would not get you where you need to be. You have to make smart decisions on the course, which is what Payne finally did.

—————

Before the season got under way, Payne made it clear to Earl Stewart, a former PGA Tour player, that he wasn't satisfied with his past results. **Kyle O'Brien-Stevens**, *a member of the SMU women's golf team in the late 1970s who later played on the LPGA Tour until her career was prematurely curtailed by back injuries, explains:*

Payne went into Earl Stewart's office and said, "I'm going to play for you this year. This is going to be my year." They had the kind of conversation that Coach Stewart had always been wanting to have with Payne because he had so much talent. Coach was very happy for him. And then Payne went out and played the type of golf he should have been playing the whole time.

I wasn't surprised, really. I had seen the serious side of Payne before. I remember on the way back from a tournament in Albuquerque—the women's and men's teams had played on the same course that day—I sat next to him on the plane. We were having a great chat about life in general. I took away from that conversation that he wasn't just a guy who liked to have a good time. He was a Fiji, and I was a Theta, and we hung out together a lot. He also, believe it or not, could be pretty humble. On that same flight, a few of the stewardesses addressed everyone before we got to Dallas, saying that it had been a long day and, being a little giddy, they had decided to award "the Fox of the Night," and it was going to the gentleman in 7D, or whatever seat Payne was in. It wasn't a big shock; he was, after all, an extremely good-looking man. They gave him a bottle of champagne. He took it like a champ. He wasn't arrogant about it in the least, just showing his cute grin.

With Earl Stewart as Payne's new mentor, his prior one, **Sam Reynolds**, *was pleased. He knew that Payne was in excellent hands:*

When I heard that Earl Stewart was the golf coach at SMU, I bubbled inside. I knew this guy; he was another Tommy Bolt [the highly talented, if volatile, 1958 U.S. Open champion]. Earl was a perfectionist. If he missed a shot, he would [get really upset]. He was just as mad as Tommy Bolt. Payne couldn't have gotten involved with a better person. Boy, what a player Earl Stewart was! He won everything as an amateur down in Texas. Payne had his father, then me, and then Earl Stewart. The basic fundamentals of his swing had been created, as well as his ability to be competitive.

—◄◄◄ ◊ ►►►—

One of the biggest events of Payne's senior season was the 1979
Southwest Conference Championship at Briarwood Golf Club in
Tyler, Texas, although he didn't seem too anxious about it, accord-
ing to former SMU sports information director **Bob Condron**, *who*
gave him a ride from Dallas:

He was taking a final that day, so he wasn't able to make
the team bus. It took us about an hour and a half to get
there. We had a great time, talking mostly about sports,
which wasn't surprising. Payne was such a huge sports fan.
I couldn't help but notice how relaxed he was during that
whole trip, not nervous in the least. He was to [soon] play
in the Southwest Conference championship. You would
have thought that he was on his way to get something to
eat. My son, who was just a kid at the time, still talks
about that day like it was yesterday. He was so impressed
with Payne.

—◄◄◄ ◊ ►►►—

More than twenty years later, what happened in Tyler on that
spring afternoon still stands out among the players and fans who
were fortunate enough to attend. It turned out to be a preview of
the future, as Payne and Fred Couples battled each other for indi-
vidual honors. At stake, for the winner, was more than conference
bragging rights. At stake was an invitation to the prestigious Colo-
nial National Invitation Tournament several weeks later in Fort
Worth. CBS announcer **Jim Nantz**, *Couples's former roommate*
at the University of Houston, provides background:

By my sophomore year, I was traveling with the team.
Coach [Dave] Williams saw me almost as his assistant.

So I would walk with the team during the big events, which is how I happened to watch Payne closely for the first time. He played wonderfully that day. But after Fred birdied eighteen [he missed an eagle putt] to tie him, it meant that Fred was the winner. There was an actual rule at the time, that to emphasize the team aspect of the whole event, there would be no play-off if there was a tie at the end of the individual competition. Instead, they would settle it by matching cards, going backward from eighteen, which is how Fred was the winner [Couples had parred fourteen; Payne had bogeyed it]. But afterward, there seemed to be a movement afoot that since Fred was a sophomore and Payne a senior, the two ought to have a play-off for the right to go to Colonial. Fred didn't have to do it but he did. He said, "Let's go play off. I'll have other years." Which, of course, he would.

In the play-off, Couples was facing an underachiever with no history of winning big matches. But, as Payne had told Earl Stewart, this was the year to start a new history. On the first play-off hole, he hit the fairway while Couples missed it right, leading to an eventual bogey. With a par, the championship belonged to Payne, along with the berth to the Colonial. Payne didn't do much with that berth, recording rounds of 74 and 76 at Colonial Country Club to miss the cut by five shots. Nonetheless, he gained a few admirers that week, including 1969 U.S. Amateur champion, **Steve Melnyk**:

I hadn't heard anything about him before that. I think there were only one or two amateurs in the field. He had wonderful manners. I introduced myself to him one day. He said, "Yes, sir," and "No, sir." When I first saw him play that week, there was sort of a cross between a wonderful grace and style with his swing combined with a little swagger, even as an amateur. It was really nice to see. He was borderline cocky, but you kind of knew that this was a kid who was different.

—————

*A few weeks later, the scene was the 1979 Missouri Amateur at Wolf Creek Golf Links just outside Kansas City, and Payne was one of the favorites. He didn't take long to show why, eliminating one opponent after another on his way to a seemingly inevitable appointment in the finals with defending champion Jim Holtgrieve, a member of the victorious U.S. Walker Cup squad. But it isn't the golf that people remember from their duel; it's the gamesmanship. Holtgrieve's caddie, **Tom O'Toole Jr.**, relays what occurred:*

It was really the night before, on Saturday night, in the parking lot when things started to get a little ugly. Payne made some comment to Jim, something to the tune of "Bring your best game, tomorrow, big boy." And, Holtgrieve, who was a hard-nosed guy and a little heavy at the time, wasn't too pleased by this kid. Jim was about ten years older. Anyway, they came face to face, and I had to get between the two of them. Otherwise, there might have been an altercation right there.

—————

This treasured picture represents the six Missouri state amateur champions who came out of Hickory Hills Country Club. At top left is 1991 state champ Alan Rosen; top right is Wayne Frederick (1996); bottom right is Chuck Greene (1998); bottom left is Bruce Hollowell (1975); center is Payne Stewart (1979); and Payne is holding a photo of his dad, Bill Stewart (1953 and 1957). (Photo courtesy of Bruce Hollowell)

Bruce Hollowell, *who had lost to Holtgrieve 6&5 in the semifinals, offered Payne some advice for the big confrontation:*

I hung around after my match to make sure he was winning and also because I wanted to help him. He was young and scared to death. When I went to see Payne, he said, "My God, how am I going to beat this guy?" because Jim was an awfully good player, probably a better player than Payne. For about ten or fifteen minutes, I told him a couple of things to do that I thought could help him win. Jim was pretty cocky about how wonderful he was. I just told Payne to get up there and make fun of his girth. Jim thought of himself as God's gift to women, and I told Payne to let him know that he's not. He said, "You really want me to do that?" I said, "You bet. You'll get him so mad that he won't be able to draw it back," and so that's what he did. Payne later mentioned to me that if it hadn't been for what I had said to him, "I would have been so sweet and nice." I also let him know that this guy had shot four or five under against me and he wasn't going to do that two days in a row. When you blister the course like that, you're usually fighting against it the next time.

—⟨⟩—

*Understandably, **Jim Holtgrieve**, who plays on the Senior PGA Tour these days, was quite perturbed with the way Payne acted. His antics only made him more determined to teach this upstart a lesson. But this upstart, at least on this particular day, was the one who did all the teaching. Holtgrieve remembers:*

Payne was basically a cocky kid. I had played in front of him during qualifying on the first day and it went very slow. He blamed me for the slow play. I told him it wasn't me, but we kind of got into it in the parking lot. He said that I was an old man and it was time for me to move on. He was very disrespectful. I was the reigning state champion and a good friend of his father's. You could tell he had come to win and take over amateur golf in the state of Missouri and wasn't afraid to let anyone know about it. I didn't appreciate that attitude. I don't think it would have come to fisticuffs, but there were certainly some tempers flying. Unfortunately, for me, he had the game to put behind his words, and beat me 8&7. He played phenomenally. I was five down after five holes. He was three or four under. I was worried about just getting to the afternoon of a thirty-six-hole final. It was the most humiliating loss of my golf career, and it came at the end of a verbal controversy that was very embarrassing for me. But to Payne's credit, when I saw him a few years later at his first Masters [1983], he came over to talk to me. He didn't really apologize per se, but it was clear that he felt he had acted improperly, even saying something to the effect that his father would be happy that we were talking. It was my understanding that his father was embarrassed by the way Payne had behaved back in 1979. So whenever I saw him after that, he always made a point to be gracious, to see how I was doing. He grew up a lot over the years.

CHASING A DREAM

Payne told me that his dad's motto was always to leave them knowing that you were in the room. He said he had adopted that philosophy.

—GARY McCORD,
TV GOLF COMMENTATOR

After finally attaining the success at SMU that many had long anticipated, the big man on campus was ready for the big move—to the PGA Tour. First, however, in November 1979 Payne had to make it through the tour's Qualifying School, which, as usual, promised to be the sternest entrance exam for any professional sport. For four long days at Waterwood National CC, about seventy-five miles northeast of Houston, he would have to compete among 120 players for only twenty-seven precious spots. No wonder players always find it amusing when they're asked about the pressure of playing on the PGA Tour. Nothing during a regular tournament, they know, will ever be as agonizing as what they experienced at Q-School. They dread ever going back. "It's the toughest experience in golf," says

PGA Tour journeyman Kelly Gibson, who has made several trips. "You see players crying, wives crying. The pressure is almost physically painful. You have to think all week about what you eat and whether you can keep it down."[3]

An errant shot here, a careless three-putt there, and their whole futures might be different. Instead of squaring off against the best players in the world, with millions up for grabs, they might be stuck on some minitour in the middle of nowhere, scraping for an extra thousand bucks or so. Instead of being pampered with courtesy cars and luxurious hotel accommodations, they might have to share rides and rooms in order to save every cent possible.

Payne didn't fare too well in his first try. He was in trouble right from the start, shooting a six-over 77. Yet because of the course's difficulty—it was dubbed "Pine Valley West," after the difficult Pine Valley layout in New Jersey—he still had a chance to secure his playing privileges, even after subsequent rounds of 76 and 78. He then recorded his best round of the week, a two-over 73. Unfortunately, his best wasn't quite good enough. Payne finished at twenty-over 304, two strokes away from earning his card. The dream had to be put on hold.

———

*Payne roomed that week with Kansas City native **Mike Peck**, someone he had known from their days in junior golf. They had been teammates in best-ball competition. Peck describes the tension:*

There was definitely a do-or-die mentality that week in Texas. Thankfully, rooming with someone you were friends with helped ease the pain of all the pressure we felt. A few weeks earlier, Payne and I had traveled up to Chicago together, which was the first leg of the qualifying process. We played, ironically enough, at Kemper Lakes, where he would win the PGA exactly ten years later. The weather was so bad that week—temperatures were in the thirties—that it was a torture test. Both of us made it through relatively easily, which is when we made plans to go to the finals together. At Waterwood, I saw him in the evenings hanging around the condo, cooking some meals. It was such an emotionally grinding week that we were all going to bed at nine or ten o'clock. I can still vividly remember how long and difficult that golf course was and how hard the conditions were. The scores were very high. Waterwood, at that time, was probably the most challenging course I had ever played, and I had played all around the country. When Payne didn't qualify, I just remember how disappointed he was. I know he probably thought that he should have made it. I don't think he had even considered the possibility that he wasn't going to be playing on the tour. There weren't many people around who Payne thought were better than he was. He was very gracious, though, to me when I qualified, and he genuinely congratulated some of the other people who made it.

—————

While future PGA Tour players such as Chip Beck, Scott Hoch, John Cook, and Mike Donald earned exemptions for the 1980 season, Payne was forced to search for other places to play. But, as usual, according to **Perry Leslie**, *Payne was not discouraged for long:*

Missing at Qualifying School had never been part of the overall plan. But he wasn't down like you might have expected someone in his position to be. His response was: "What's next? I'll get them next time." That's the way he was, and that's what made him so great. And let me tell you, he was great, even if he didn't get through Q-School his first time. A lot of very talented players fail Q-School at one point or another. So Payne decided to play the mini-tour in California. He entered four tournaments and did beautifully, finishing first, second, and first in his last three. I wasn't surprised. I had seen him playing in a pro-am in Kansas City just before he was about to turn pro. He hit a couple of wedge shots that I hadn't seen in the years [1974–1978] I played the tour. I came back and told his dad, "He's not just going to be good. He's going to be great!" His dad was beaming. That's all Bill Stewart ever wanted for his kid. Bill always wanted to be a pro. This was an opportunity for Payne to live out Bill's dream, and everybody around Springfield knew that.

In California, Payne hooked up with **Mark Wiebe**, *another aspiring young professional. Wiebe, who would also one day make it to the promised land, describes one of Payne's unique habits:*

Payne had this white bag tag, and in a black sharpie, one side said, "Think," and the other side of the tag said, "Tempo." There were many times in these minitour events when Payne would be getting ready to hit and because something wasn't right, he would stop and walk over to his bag. He would take that bag tag in his hand, read one side, flip it over and read the other. Then he would come back and start his whole routine all over again. It showed a lot of mental discipline, but that's the kind of guy he was, from the time I met him when we were amateurs back in Dallas until the day he died.

———

Payne could accomplish only so much in California, and, unfortunately, in the early 1980s, there was no Nike Tour or Hooters Tour or Golden Bear Tour for players to polish their games as they waited for their next crack at Qualifying School. So Payne settled on another option—the Asian Tour. It was an option that **Jim Morris** *said made a lot of sense:*

If you get over to the Asian Tour and you have some capabilities and you're playing every week, it takes a lot of pressure off of you, and that was obviously the thought of Payne's sponsors, all of whom were from Springfield. Bill had told him to go out and raise the money in order that he could go on the PGA Tour. Bill said, "You go out and get five guys and I'll put up my share. See if they think you are capable of playing on the PGA Tour." Which is what he did. It was a cakewalk. Each sponsor put up about five thousand dollars, and Payne used some of that money for the Asian Tour. Let me tell you, there wasn't much disappointment on anybody's part when he didn't get through the Qualifying School, and that includes me. I knew how good he was. I knew from the way he played Hickory Hills. Hickory Hills is a great golf course. You could hold a U.S. Open there. If you go around that course every time in sixty-six or sixty-seven strokes, you can make it on the tour. I've never seen anybody do that, except Payne.

———

Joined by wife Tracey and daughter Chelsea, then five, Payne celebrates his 1991 U.S. Open triumph after beating Scott Simpson in an eighteen-hole play-off at Hazeltine National Golf Club in Chaska, Minnesota. (AP/Wide World Photos; Morry Gash)

Payne enjoyed tremendous success on the Asian Tour. He cap-
tured the Indonesian Open and the Indian Open, and finished
third on the Asian Order of Merit. But he found much more than
a golf game in Asia. He found love. Her name was Tracey Fergu-
son. Tracey was on vacation to watch her brother, Mike, play in
the 1980 Malaysian Open when she spotted Payne for the first
time at a cocktail party. Tracey, says longtime friend **Todd Awe***,*
was exactly what Payne needed:

He told us all about this wonderful person he had met,
and how they knew that they were meant for each other.
I remember him describing her as a beautiful woman, and
that he couldn't wait to get married and bring her over to
the States to start their new life together. They had such
a great relationship. I think Tracey gave Payne something
to really play for. Payne wanted to please her and have
success for her.

I don't think Payne would have traded those years
for anything. Neither of us were big letter writers, but
every time he would come home, we'd meet somewhere.
He thought Asia was fascinating. He couldn't believe the
poverty that existed in some of the areas. I think Jakarta
[the capital of Indonesia] was one area in particular that
really got to him a little bit. I think it made him feel
really grateful for his blessings, as opposed to feeling sorry
for himself that he had to play in Asia.

During the 1999 memorial service for Payne in Orlando, **Tracey**
Stewart *spoke about the first time she and Payne saw each other:*

He was the most beautiful-looking man I had ever seen. It
was love at first sight. He always told me it was the same

for him, and that we were destined to be together. I truly believe that, too. Even though I didn't meet Payne till a few days later, I remember thinking about this person I hadn't even met yet. I didn't even know what his name was. We played our games with each other for several days until, finally, another golfer introduced us. We talked for a brief couple of minutes before I had to leave. The next morning in the clubhouse, before the round, I was there with my brother. Payne finally gained enough courage to ask me out to dinner that night. I acted non-chalant about it. Meanwhile, inside, I was screaming with joy. From the night of the first date, I can honestly tell you that I knew that this was the man that I wanted to share my life with. . . . Even after eighteen years of marriage, Payne was still the most beautiful man I had ever seen, not because of the way he looked on the outside anymore, but because of what was on the inside.[4]

—◦—

Jim Morris believes it's impossible to overestimate the role Tracey played in Payne's career, especially in the beginning when the future was so uncertain. As much as Morris had confidence in the ability of Bill Stewart's son, he was not entirely convinced that he could harness it in the appropriate manner. Until, that is, Tracey came along:

My only concern about Payne was his discipline. I had no doubt that he could make it on the tour, and believe me, I sponsored some boys I knew who couldn't make it. But I was concerned about the discipline side of him. He had a happy-go-lucky attitude, but he had that one disciplined side and that one undisciplined side. That's where Tracey came in. Marrying her was a big step toward his becoming a real professional. She helped him develop that disciplined side, and I knew that if that side took over, Payne Stewart was going to be as good a professional as would come down the pike. If there was a tiller, she was the steady on the tiller. He achieved things on his own the last three or four years of his life, but in the years when he was wobbling a little bit, she was that steadiness that was always there for him, when it was hard for him to settle down.

———

Golf writer **Greg Stoda**, *who used to make bets with Payne during the NBA play-offs, says that Tracey was the one sure thing in his life that made him a better man:*

I don't think a lot of people knew how much Payne depended on Tracey, including Payne. At his worst times and his best times, he was the life-of-the-party guy. I think Tracey tempered that slightly just by her presence. I think she was the one who could tell Payne things that nobody else could tell him. I always got the impression that Tracey knew best, and he knew that Tracey knew best.

———

Bee Payne-Stewart *will never forget when her son first mentioned the girl he found on the other side of the world:*

He brought this picture home with him and said, "Oh, look at this girl I met over in Asia. Isn't she beautiful?" That was Payne—anybody he loved, they were beautiful. He didn't talk about marriage. He wasn't even on the [PGA] tour yet. He didn't have any way to support her.

But he did have her come over here. She came to our house before they were married and stayed here for a while. We made her feel right at home. We had everybody come to meet her, and I had receptions for her. They had a beautiful wedding in Australia. Her folks went all out. She was Catholic and Payne was Methodist, so she had it in a Methodist church. It was very expensive to go that far, so just Bill and I went over there.

—◁◆▷—

After conquering Asia, Payne returned to America to prepare for his fourth attempt at Q-School [he had failed in both his second and third efforts in 1980]. This time, though, in the spring of 1981, he finally passed. Shooting a six-under 282 on the Palm Course at Walt Disney World in Lake Buena Vista, Florida, Payne earned his ticket to the big leagues. He would never need one again. **Mark Wiebe** *roomed with him that week:*

I remember the phone call Payne made to Tracey that night in Australia after he knew he was going to get his card. He said, "Hey, I made it. Let's get married." That was their plan—to get married and then go out on the tour. He was pretty excited. He also called his dad; I don't remember what he said to him. The funniest thing that happened that week, though, was when we were watching these storms come through. One of them came through pretty bad. We were outside watching it from real high up in this hotel, when I said to Payne, "Well, that's enough for me," and I went inside. He didn't follow me right away. He said, "Hey, Weeb, if it's your time to go, it's your time to go." I said, "Yeah, well, I don't have to force that." He stood there and looked at me. He said, "You know what, you're right," then he closed the slider and came in. We both laughed.

—◦◦◦—

A card in those days, however, did not guarantee entry into PGA Tour events. Players were still required to go through a round of Monday qualifying to get into that week's field. After several misses, Payne finally cashed his first check, for $1,031, when he finished in a tie for fifty-eighth in the British Open at Royal St. George's. A few months later, at the Southern Open in Columbus, Georgia, he got into serious contention for the first time. It showed. Sharing the lead heading into Sunday, he faltered with a 73, including bogeys on the last three holes, to finish in a tie for ninth. Nonetheless, as **Perry Leslie** *points out, confidence was never one of Payne's problems:*

When he first got on the tour, he was a little cocky. In fact, he was downright arrogant, and it really affected people. He never could say the right thing in front of the camera. Of course, the people in Springfield kind of dismissed a lot of it because he was our boy. We didn't like to see anybody put him down. But a few of us would get on him a little bit about it. I said, "America doesn't want to hear how good you think you are. What they want to hear is that it could happen to anyone. They want to hear that the dream exists for them. They want to hear humility." After all the time we had spent together over the years, I felt like I certainly had the authority to say this to him. Also, I was the only person he knew who had experienced the tour on a regular basis. I played for several years in the 1970s. He listened to almost every word I said.

—◄◄◄◄◄►►►►►—

*In April 1982, less than a year after he had finally made it through Q-School, Payne won the Magnolia Classic in Hattiesburg, Mississippi, an unofficial event played on the same week as the Masters. Three months later, again while the game's best players were occupied elsewhere—this time in the British Open at Royal Troon—he captured the Quad Cities Open. This victory was official. Two decades later, **Brad Bryant**, who finished in a tie for second at Quad Cities, two shots behind Payne, still sounds a bit overwhelmed when recounting the final round:*

On fifteen Payne made about an eighteen-foot putt. On sixteen, he made about a twenty-five-foot putt that had about six feet of break. Then, on seventeen, he made a fifty-footer that hit the back of the hole, popped up, and went in. It looked like it was going to go about six or seven feet by. It was pretty amazing watching him make all these long putts. As we were going down fourteen or fifteen, my wife, Sue, went over and said hello to Tracey. Tracey was just a bundle of nerves, so as they're walking down toward the green, she was so nervous that she looked at Sue and said, "I'm sorry, I can't talk right now. I just have to be able to concentrate." We all thought that was perfect, that it kind of characterized those early years with Payne and Tracey, how you hardly ever saw one without the other.

—◄◄◄◄◄►►►►►—

In between those two victories, Payne made a choice that would define his career forever. It had nothing to do with his caddie or his clubs; it had everything to do with his clothes. For the third round of the Atlanta Classic, in the same state that produced Bobby Jones,

*he put on a pair of knickers, the traditional wardrobe golfers donned
in the 1920s and 1930s. Payne got the idea on the driving range
one day when he realized he was wearing almost the exact same
outfit as another player. For someone who strove so fervently to be
different, this was a problem. Remembering how sharp Stewart
Ginn and Rodger Davis had looked with knickers on the Asian
Tour, he figured it might just work for him, as well. It turned out to
be a brilliant career move, providing Payne with the identity—and
marketing power—that most players, such as his friend **Mark Lye**,
could probably never imagine:*

I understand now why he wore that ugly crap from the
Tampa Bay Buccaneers to the Chicago Bears. It gave him
something that nobody else on the planet could do. He
had a way of getting people to recognize him. I once said
to him, "Man, if you're going to dress like that, you better
have some game to back it up, buddy, or they're going to
laugh you right off the tour." He says, "Don't worry about
me, I've got plenty of game." I remember once, he had a
party at Bay Hill when Chelsea [the Stewarts' daughter]
was an infant. I had never been to his house. I couldn't
believe how big his closet was. It was like the length of
the room on both sides. It was so bright you had to have
your sunglasses on to go in there.

---

*Some of his colleagues on tour were curious about the knickers,
especially once they realized that this was no temporary gimmick.
They wanted to know more. One day, **Gary McCord**, a flashy
player in his own right, asked him:*

I was in Springfield to do his pro-am. He had just started
on the tour and had just begun to wear the knickers. We

were on him so bad for wearing those things. That night, when we were at a cocktail party, just talking, I said to him, "What is it with those knickers?" He goes, "When I was younger, my dad was a door-to-door salesman and he always had a flair. He had the worst collection of ugly coats you have ever seen." Payne told me that his dad's motto was always to leave them knowing that you were in the room. He said he had adopted that philosophy.

—⟨⟩—

*His style of dress wasn't the only distinction that separated Payne from the pack. So did his membership over the years in Jake Trout and the Flounders, a band comprised of tour players Peter Jacobsen, Mark Lye, and Larry Rinker. As **Mark Lye** recalls, Payne, who played the harmonica and sang some backup, was a big hit:*

In our band, he was the star. When we were shooting our video, me and Peter were there, along with about fifty other people in Los Angeles. At about eight o'clock in the morning, we're wondering: "Where the heck is Payne?" Finally, he gets there at nine o'clock. He looks at himself in front of the mirror and says, "You know, my hair is just a little long. Can somebody get someone down here to cut my hair?" So we had to get someone down there to do the shampoo and cut his hair. Afterwards, he says, "Okay, I feel good now." And then he puts his hat on! You can't see his hair! That was Payne.

—⟨⟩—

Payne thrived on being the center of attention, whether he was in front of the gallery at a course or the audience at a club. Tour professional **Andrew Magee** *was often around to watch his friend perform:*

We used to find ourselves on stage with Duck Soup, a band from Austin, Texas. Payne and I would always go up there. I was always a little nervous until I had a few beers. But Payne was never nervous. He loved getting in front of people and playing his harmonica, no matter how good or bad he was. He would go right up in the front. The head guy would say, "What do you want to do?" And Payne would say, "Man, I know everything. Let's get going." He showed me that a tour pro could go out and have a good time the night before and still win tournaments. You didn't have to just sit in your hotel room, read books, and go to bed early to play great golf.

On one occasion, Payne's nerves did catch up to him. It was in Memphis when Jack Trout and the Flounders were preparing to record their first album. **Peter Jacobsen** *tells the story:*

I picked him up in the airport and drove him over. He had his harmonica out and started to play along. He couldn't do it. He said, "I'm so nervous." So we sent a couple of production assistants out to the local 7-Eleven for a few "beverages." We sat in the back of the rental car and we drank a few ice-cold "beverages." I think Payne had four; I had two. Payne played as smooth as he ever played. He put his dark sunglasses on.[5]

---

*Yet as much as he thoroughly enjoyed his music, Payne knew when it was time to turn down the volume to concentrate on his golf game. It was a balancing act that **Mark Lye** found very impressive:*

The times at golf tournaments were sacred. You couldn't mess with him; he was able to focus. A lot of people can't turn it off and turn it on, but that's what he was able to do. He went to the course every day with more intensity than anybody. He had to get there earlier. He had to get loosened up. If he had a noon tee time, he was there at nine and if he had a seven o'clock tee time, he was there at five. He worked hard. When you played a practice round with him, he would hit it from every possible location, out of every bunker. I'd go to his caddie [Mike Hicks] and say, "Hicksy, I can't practice with this guy. He's wearing me out." He said, "How do you think I feel?" Funniest thing I ever remember, I went to an Orlando Magic game when Payne shot some baskets for a charity. They had a clock on him; he looked like a chicken with his head cut off. He did lay-ups and shot from different spots around the key. I said, "Man, why did you do it?" He said, "I know I looked like a jerk but it was fun," and he made some money for charity.

---

*Indeed, those moments on the golf course were very sacred. **Brad Bryant** reflects on a special routine Payne and Tracey followed that would make a big difference in the years ahead:*

In the early 1980s Payne worked harder on his putting than anybody I have ever known. He would get about ten golf balls together and surround the hole about eight feet away. Tracey would line them up. She would then just sit there and watch him for hours. It was really something. He was an extremely bold player, especially with his putting. He made great putts under tremendous amounts of pressure and I think all of the real hard practice that Payne did early in his career paid off.

———

Even eleven-time tour winner **Andy Bean**, *who probably envisioned himself as a pretty hard worker, was very impressed with the effort from Payne and Tracey he observed one day:*

One of the first times I paid much attention to him was at the Los Angeles Open in 1983 at Riviera Country Club. He and Tracey were on the putting green while I was practicing my putting. I was there for at least another hour or so, and they were still there. Just about when Payne had gone all the way around the circle for the second or third time, he asked if she was ready to get something to eat. Tracey looked at him and said, "I think you need to work on these a little bit more." I thought that was great. I think that really said a lot about both of them.

———

Another member of Payne's team was his caddie, **Mitch Kemper**. *Kemper, who now works as executive director for a Southern California investment firm, carried Payne's bags during much of the 1982 and 1983 seasons. He still gets excited when the subject turns to the man who played such a prominent role in his life:*

I'll always remember during the Monday practice round at the Masters in 1983 [Payne's first], when we got to around the third hole, he said, "Bud, you have got to put the bag down and hit shots with me. This is unbelievable." Payne just had to have me hit some shots. That's the kind of guy he was. He treated me like a champ. So I played holes three through eight. I had to stop before we got too close to the clubhouse because we could have gotten in trouble.

He always wanted what was best for me. At the Tournament of Champions at La Costa, he said, "I think you should do something else with your life." I said, "What are you talking about?" He said, "You're very gifted in the stock market. I'm going to give you some money. I want you to go to Santa Barbara and become a stockbroker." I told him I had never had a regular job like that in my life, and he said, "If you can't make it, you can come rejoin me in a month. I really think you should give this a try." He said, "I'm firing you as my caddie but not as my friend." That was his famous line. Yet I was pretty [ticked] off at him. We went through a difficult period. But to make a long story short, I eventually got my license in the securities business, and Payne opened up a $5,000 pension plan with me for one of my first three accounts. From that time on, I've built a very good career in which I handle famous clients. He was my backbone the whole way.

———

*Speaking of caddies, Payne needed one for the 1984 British Open at the famed Old Course in St. Andrews, Scotland. He brought his good friend **Todd Awe**. Payne, however, first had to make it through an initial stage of qualifying to secure a spot in the game's oldest major championship. Awe looks back:*

He didn't have a full-time caddie or a caddie who would risk a plane ticket to London, hoping that Payne would get into the tournament. So my wife and I went over to St. Andrews with Payne and Tracey. He did qualify, and we had a wonderful time, renting a small house in town. He related so well to the people over there. Back then at the British Open, they had a cut after three rounds. On the last hole, which is a very short par-four, he knew he was right on the cut line. He hit a wonderful drive, and with a wedge, went right at the hole. The ball actually hit the pin but, unluckily, kicked back to the front of the green and down into the Valley of the Sin. Instead of a real close chance for a birdie, he failed to get it up and down for a par and wound up missing the cut by a single shot.

GETTING OVER THE HUMP

Trying to describe his swing, breaking it down in clinical terms, would be like trying to describe how a Rolls-Royce runs. I always said that about Payne, that he had a swing like a Rolls-Royce. All you had to do was be sure that the water and oil levels were right, and that there was gasoline in the car.

**—E. HARVIE WARD,
SWING COACH**

Near misses soon became pretty common for Payne—so common, in fact, that in the mid-1980s, he was branded as "Avis." Time and time again, he would seize the lead in a tournament, and time and time again, he would let it slip away. Something would happen—an errant drive, a shaky three-putt, something—and the winner's trophy would be awarded to someone else. From 1984 through 1986, he recorded six second-place finishes and twenty-eight top-10s, but not a single victory. In 1986 he earned what was then the most money—$535,389—ever earned by a player without a victory.

Two examples stand out from this frustrating period. Both, ironically enough, took place in the Dallas-Fort Worth area. In the first, the 1984 Colonial National Invitation Tournament, Payne led by one stroke going into the final hole. But his drive on the dogleg left went far right, stopping on a muddy downslope, just three feet short of a man-made stream and right beside a cement pedestrian bridge. He had no shot to the green, closing with a bogey that put him in a play-off with Peter Jacobsen. On the first play-off hole, Payne again hit it right. His second shot went through the green. Jacobsen, meanwhile, hit a wedge to within six feet. Game, set and match, Mr. Jacobsen.

The second collapse was even harder to comprehend. At the 1985 Byron Nelson Classic, Payne led by two as he teed off on eighteen. All he had to do was bogey the hole and he would win the tournament. It would be a popular win, as well, coming in front of fans and friends from his days at nearby SMU. But Payne proceeded to hit three straight shots into bunkers, two-putting from eighteen feet for a double bogey that put him in another play-off, this one with Bob Eastwood. If that wasn't humiliating enough, he then double bogeyed the first play-off hole.

———

The loss to Eastwood remains memorable. It wasn't merely the manner in which Payne blew the tournament. It was also because of a particularly poignant camera shot that CBS aired of Payne and Tracey after the play-off was over, a shot that, according to senior associate producer **Chuck Will**, *even Payne grew to value:*

The tournament ended at about ten to 6:00 P.M. East Coast time, and as was the practice at CBS, our cameramen didn't just bag up because we were finished with golf. So all of a sudden, I looked up in the truck and saw this wonderful full-frame picture of Payne and Tracey with their arms around each other behind the green. You couldn't see their faces, only their backs. We showed it on the air, and people loved it. A few weeks later, I was on an airplane when I felt a hand on my shoulder. It was Payne. He had heard about this shot and wanted to get a copy of it. So I sent one to him. Years later I ran into him while we were both being treated for back problems, and he said, "Do you remember that shot?" Of course, I remembered it. He then told me, "We [he and Tracey] break that thing out and look at it pretty often." To me, it shows that the picture of him and Tracey together meant more to him than the painful memory of losing a golf tournament.

---

*Naturally, losing the golf tournament did hurt a great deal, although, in the process, Payne picked up a new admirer, **Byron Nelson**, who would become a friend:*

That was really the first time I got acquainted with him. He conducted himself very well in a situation, of course, where he had to be feeling terrible after really just throwing the tournament away. But he didn't act that way. He didn't complain about it or act ugly. He just said, "Well, I hit some bad shots."

---

*The bad shots, which came at the worst times, happened for a reason, according to **Perry Leslie**. Analyzing Payne's performance from his home in Springfield, the Hickory Hills professional spotted a much deeper problem:*

While watching on television, I could see the stress in his face. That's why Payne didn't win a lot of those tournaments. He had the type of golf swing that was perfect and classical but required absolutely no tension. But when he came down the home stretch, almost invariably, there was tension. I could see the stress in his body and once that happened, he was finished because he needed a body that would be totally relaxed. Sometimes the stress manifested itself on the green, sometimes it manifested itself on the drives. Sometimes he just started to misclub.

Meanwhile, the news wasn't so good back in Springfield. Bill Stewart was very sick. Payne would take a break in his hectic schedule as often as possible to visit the man who had taught him so much about golf and about life. Family friend **Donna Thompson** *remembers:*

It was tough on him when his dad got cancer. He would come home and see how much Bill had deteriorated, and that hurt a lot. He felt like he needed to be here. It was hard for him to leave because he hadn't been home very much as he was playing in tournaments. But Bill, who was on chemotherapy at the time, wanted him out there playing, so he could watch him on TV.

For the first couple of years after Bill died [in 1985], it was very hard for Payne. He missed the words his father would say to him before each tournament, how Bill would be able to pump him up like nobody else could. Bill dwelled on the good things Payne did, but in the same breath, he would also say, "Now, Buss, you're dropping your shoulder on that drive." Bill was Payne's best and worst critic. He might not talk to him for a couple of days, but then he would see something on television and say, "I saw you on this hole but you did this." I can remember that when Lora [Payne's sister] and I sat with Bill to watch one tournament, he just praised Payne, talking to the TV. But, at different moments, he would say, "Remember that, Lora, so we can tell him." Maybe he had dropped his shoulder or his foot was turned the wrong way. Bill just lived and breathed for Payne's golf game. When Payne would come home, even after he had turned pro, the two of them would go to the club and find a game.

―――

*In 1986 Payne seized the lead on the back nine of the U.S. Open at Shinnecock Hills on Long Island. If he could grab a major championship victory, he would bury the "Avis" label forever. But with four bogeys in his last six holes, the label was still very much alive. Payne finished in a tie for sixth, four shots behind winner Raymond Floyd. **Jaime Diaz**, who covered the tournament for* Sports Illustrated, *describes a most revealing moment:*

When Payne was in the lead, I walked out to the thirteenth hole. He had a birdie chip from off the green, ran it about six feet by, and missed it coming back. He was playing with Floyd. They went to the next tee and there was a little portable outhouse off the tee there. Floyd went in. Payne was going to go in, so he waited for Floyd. I was just standing there. When Floyd walked out, Payne said something like, "Nice putt, Raymond," looking for some kind of acknowledgment. And Floyd stared right through him. I just remember thinking, "This guy's a little out of his depth right here." He didn't have it mentally.

―――

Over time, the failure to win tournaments, or close the deal as they say on the tour, got to Payne. He wasn't alone. One day, Tracey Stewart phoned **Paul Celano**, *director of golf at Grand Cypress in Orlando. Celano recalls their conversation:*

She said, "Paul, we have got to do something. What can we do to help him get over the hump? It's really tearing him up." I said I had somebody in mind and that was Harvie Ward. He was my mentor. I thought that Payne needed to know how to win. Harvie is one of only two people to win the United States, Canadian, and British Amateurs. Harvie beat Nicklaus in the National Amateur [1958]. Mr. Hogan used to ask to play with him at Augusta. Payne needed a coach who could help him with handling pressure, of knowing what to do in certain situations. Harvie taught him how to play when the heat was on.

―――

E. Harvie Ward *welcomed the chance to work with such a promising, if undisciplined, player. With his credentials, Ward didn't hesitate to tell his new student exactly what was necessary for him to become a big-time player:*

I taught Payne for about two years, from 1987 through 1989. When I first saw him, I immediately thought he had a lot of talent and that there wasn't going to be too much for me to do. I'd say to him, "What do you think about this?" or "What do you think about that?" It wasn't, "You ought to do this" or "You ought to do that." You don't start talking about mechanics with people who have a natural swing. The only thing you had to worry about with him was the timing, getting the club down to meet the movement of his body. I didn't work on trying to reshape his swing. Trying to describe his swing, breaking it down in clinical terms, would be like trying to describe how a Rolls-Royce runs. I always said that about Payne, that he had a swing like a Rolls-Royce. All you had to do was be sure that the water and oil levels were right and that there was gasoline in the car. Then you just point him in the right direction and watch him go. He was a little stubborn at times. He didn't like any changes. If you suggested something to him about his swing, he was a little reluctant, so you didn't want to push him too much.

I did work with him on his attitude. I won't say it was bad, but in a lot of ways he was a little immature. He liked to do funny things. But because he hit the ball so well, it didn't reflect that much in his scores, although he probably could have been better years earlier if he had shown just a little more maturity. I'm not referring so much in terms of golf management. It was just that he took things a little too lightly. It didn't look like he was really into it. If you compare him to, say, a Tiger Woods, you'd be talking about night and day. Tiger is so tenacious. Payne never gave you that idea.

Not that he wouldn't try. It was just his attitude toward the game. Payne thought, "The game is fun," instead of, "The game is work and the game is my livelihood. I've got to treat it like a doctor who goes to the hospital to operate on somebody." He didn't seem to feel that way. He didn't come across like he wanted to win all the four majors. If he won, fine. If he didn't win, it wasn't the end of the world. That's why I introduced him to Dr. Richard Coop [a professor of educational psychology at the University of North Carolina–Chapel Hill]. I wasn't a psychologist. I could say things to him, but I felt that if he went to a golf psychologist, he could get to Payne a lot better than I could.

Payne and I would generally work in the morning, and then sometimes play in the afternoon. We played with Paul Azinger, Andy Bean, Mark O'Meara. We worked together probably three or four times a week. I tried to keep getting him more into the game, to pay more attention, rather than being kind of lackadaisical. He was coming along very well. But to get to the next level, he needed something I couldn't give him.

I also worked with him on the pace of his swing. He seemed to overswing sometimes, letting the club drop a little bit at the top and then he would have trouble getting back to the ball. So I was trying to get him to get the club to the top of his swing to where it was parallel and not go past parallel, because that's when he would get a little wild. As long as he kept the club at parallel and not beyond, he kept the ball in play much better.

At one time, he was not putting very well. If he had an Achilles heel, it would have been his putting. When he got under the gun, he had a tendency to pick the putter up and a little outside instead of keeping it low. When you pick it up, you tend to take it outside and cut the ball. I was reasonably successful with him. I tried to have him keep the putter down and if you do that, you keep it on line.

In a way, I think I was kind of a father figure to him, though he'd never admit it. He never said it specifically to me, but Paul [Celano] told me that Payne felt I had helped him a lot because I had kind of taken the place of his father.

*Father figure or not, Ward showed plenty of wisdom by sending Payne to **Dr. Richard Coop**. Dr. Coop, who had worked with Ben Crenshaw and other talented players, made a big difference in Payne's career. Perhaps his biggest contribution took place years later when he helped discover that Payne suffered from Attention Deficit Disorder. Together, they worked out a strategy to cope with the problem. Dr. Coop reminisced about his star pupil:*

I first met Payne more than eleven years ago. I told him pretty bluntly about some things I had heard about him—that he was prickly, arrogant, cocky, and brash. After finishing our first session, he asked, "Can I use your phone?" He called Tracey and she asked what had transpired. Payne told her what I had said and she asked him, "What do you think?" He said, "He's probably right." That's how we started what was to become not only a rewarding work relationship but a close friendship that I will always treasure. That first meeting was significant because it became the nature of our relationship. I was always frank with Payne about everything. He didn't always like it at the time, but later he would come back and admit that what I had said had some merit. He didn't want to come see me at first. Harvie pushed him. And if we hadn't had some early success, I don't believe he would have come back. In fact, he later told me that was the case.[6]

---

*In 1991, after Payne won the U.S. Open for the first time, he took **Dr. Richard Coop**, as well as his caddie Mike Hicks and swing coach Chuck Cook, for a week of golf in Scotland. Dr. Coop looks back at some moments from their memorable excursion:*

We had no reservations. We just popped into bed-and-breakfasts wherever we were. To give you an idea about how intuitive he was, he always drove our van and gave me the road map. Except we never used it. He drove around the Scottish countryside strictly by feel—and we almost never got lost. He had an amazing sense of direction. Every time we had dinner somewhere, he always included the restaurant's other patrons. One night, a group of twenty American college students followed us out the door and down the street. That's when we started calling Payne "Pied Piper." . . . Everywhere we played, fathers would bring their sons and daughters to watch Payne's beautiful, classic swing. No child could ever bother him, and he had time for each and every one.

In recent years, he talked publicly about his battle with Attention Deficit Disorder. What people don't realize is that God gave him tempo, rhythm, and feel, but he had to work very hard on his concentration. However, under the right conditions, like many ADD sufferers, he could hyperfocus. That's why he did better in majors than in the John Deere Classic, for example. He was impulsive at times (which often accompanies ADD), and he often spoke before he thought, which got him into trouble with the media. He was constantly trying to find the right level of arousal and concentration under which he could perform most effectively.[7]

---

*As Payne learned how to win, it became his turn to intimidate other players. One of those victims was **Kenny Perry**, who faced him in the final round of the 1989 MCI Heritage Classic at Hilton Head. Perry was totally overmatched:*

We were in the last group together on Saturday and Sunday. This is when he was playing some pretty awesome golf. He was one of the big stars on the tour. He won the tournament and I finished second, but I'll never forget how I was thinking, "Man, I can't beat this guy." Hilton Head is a really tight course. It was important not just to hit fairways. You have to hit the proper sides of the fairways because all of the greens have trees overhanging them. But he was pulling this old Wilson driver—it was called a whale with a red graphite shaft— on every hole. It didn't matter what hole we were on, he was hitting driver while I was hitting three-woods and one-irons. He was hitting it so straight. We were coming to the fifteenth hole, which is a tight par-five, and he pulls the driver out. There's out of bounds right and left, and he just gutted it right down the middle. I'm thinking, "Wow, I want to do that someday." It impressed me so much that in the heat of the moment, he had so much confidence to pull out that club. He went on to win by five shots. He was pretty flawless. He was also very relaxed. Even though he was very focused on playing, he was able to look into the gallery and talk to a few people. He was confident. He had that look of "Nobody's going to beat me today." And though he hit it a long way, his swing was very smooth and beautiful to watch. He never looked like he overswung the club.

—————

At the 1990 Byron Nelson Classic, Payne finally got redemption for his horrible loss five years earlier to Bob Eastwood. This time, there was no Sunday collapse in front of his devoted fans and friends. **Mark Lye** *was his playing partner:*

When we teed it up, I could tell that winning the tournament was a huge priority. He lived to win that tournament. The front nine that day was pretty intense and on the back side, he was my worst enemy. From his looks and body language, it was brutal, mortal combat, like: "This is it, man. Somebody is going to live and somebody is going to die, and I'm going to be the one who lives at all costs." So with three holes to go, we were sitting on a bench and he was smiling; he knew he was going to win. It was like: "Now everything's okay. Now we can be friends again." Heck, I wished I had been that way. I wish now that it had meant the world to me. Payne always wanted to be something special, and you can't be something special unless you win the big ones.

MAJOR TRIUMPHS AND TRIALS

I remember rooting like [crazy] for Lee Janzen on Sunday even though I didn't know Lee Janzen from a hole in the wall.

—JOHN FEINSTEIN, AUTHOR

The big ones, of course, are the four major championships, but by August of 1989, Payne had yet to win any of them. He had certainly come close—a second at the British Open in 1985 and a tie for fourth in 1987, and a tie for fifth at the 1986 PGA, as well as his loss to Raymond Floyd at the 1986 U.S. Open. Close, however, wasn't good enough, not for a player who, as Mark Lye said, wanted to be something special. At the same time, Payne was only thirty-two, and he still had one more chance—the 1989 PGA Championship—to claim a major before the decade ended. The site was Kemper Lakes Golf Club, just outside Chicago, where a decade earlier, he had made it through the Q-School regionals. Perhaps this time, he would pass an even tougher test and establish himself as one of the game's top players for the decade ahead.

The tournament started out, however, by revealing more of the past than the future. Both Arnold Palmer, fifty-nine, and Jack Nicklaus, forty-nine, were among seven players at four-under 68, only two shots out of the lead. Unfortunately, reality set in as both legends soon faded, paving the way for Mike Reid—nicknamed "Radar" for his precise shotmaking—to assume control of the championship. By late Sunday, Reid appeared headed for certain victory. But, as Payne knew all too well from his own late-round troubles, nothing in golf is ever certain. Reid quickly showed why. A bogey at sixteen was followed by a double at seventeen, including a disastrous three-putt from only fifteen feet. Reid still had a chance to tie Payne at eighteen but missed a very makeable seven-footer. For a change, someone else had fallen apart, and the title belonged to Payne. It would be unfair, though, to simply say the 1989 PGA Championship was the one that Mike Reid lost. It was also the one that Payne Stewart won, shooting an impressive 31 on the back nine, including four birdies in his last five holes.

———

*Becoming a major winner, however, did not automatically provide him with the immediate respect he might have imagined. Much of it was his own fault. While Reid was self-destructing, Payne was showing off in front of the television cameras, hardly dignified behavior in a major championship. For Payne, knowing how to act in victory—and defeat, for that matter—was still something he had to learn. It was, one might say, the next hump he would have to get over. **Greg Stoda**, who was covering the tournament for the* Dallas Times Herald, *summarizes the reaction in the press room:*

Mike Reid, a pretty much unknown guy, had just come in and had been as eloquent as anybody has ever been about losing. He had a great quote that I had never heard before. He said "Sports is life with the volume turned up," and his whole press conference was this reflective, "I'll probably never get this chance again, and God, I feel horrible about this." Well, Payne, as the winner, came in after him. In his defense, he wasn't aware that Reid had conducted this touching press conference. He was pretty much unapologetic on how he had won the tournament. He was severely criticized for his reaction to the victory, especially in the wake of how Reid lost it, because there was the sense that Reid wasn't ever going to get a chance to win a major again and Stewart, having finally broken through, was going to do exactly what he did—win more majors and become one of the game's great players. How he behaved with Reid was like the antithesis of what he did with Phil Mickelson at Pinehurst last year. Having finally won a major, he didn't care how anybody else had lost it.

—————

For sure, the victory was an emotional one for Payne, which was very evident when he went to do an interview with ABC. Long-time network golf producer **Terry Jastrow** *explains:*

It was less than an hour after he had won when he came into the announcers' booth to see us, because we were doing a special with Jack Nicklaus on the winners of all the major championships that year. Because Payne had won, we wanted to do an interview with him right away. Payne, being in the presence of Jack, and with Jack congratulating him, broke down. With all of his razzle-dazzle and style, he was a gentle and vulnerable soul. He was overwhelmed by what Nicklaus said to him. It was touching that it would matter so much to Payne. He was so human about it all.

———

Payne played well the rest of 1989, finishing second on the money list with more than $1.2 million. He actually had a chance to win the title, but lost to Tom Kite when he three-putted both the last hole and the second play-off hole of the season-ending Nabisco Championships in South Carolina. Avis was back, and in typical form. To make matters worse, after shaking hands with Kite, Payne stepped away about twenty yards from the gallery and reportedly screamed an obscenity.

*Nonetheless, his strong play continued in 1990 when he won two more tournaments and finished third on the money list. In 1991, however, a herniated disk in his neck sidelined him for ten weeks. He even had to skip Augusta, although, as **Paul Celano** recalls, Payne still had hopes up until the last minute:*

On the day before the first round, he decided he just wasn't ready. So, instead, on that Saturday, Payne, myself, Chuck Cook, and the pro, Mike Reynolds, played right across the street at Augusta Country Club. I remember we were on about the eighth hole when we looked through the fence and saw the twelfth green at Augusta National. Payne just stared at it for a while and said: "You know, I should really be there." You could tell how much it hurt that he couldn't play in the Masters. He played pretty good that day with us, but you could tell that he was hurting. He had probably made the right decision.

———

By shooting a back-nine 31 Sunday at Kemper Lakes, Payne was able to overcome Mike Reid to win the 1989 PGA Championship for his first major victory. Payne's triumph, however, still was met with criticism, with some saying he had "backed in" to the victory while others frowned on what they perceived as his excessive celebration at Reid's expense. (AP/Wide World Photos; Bill Waugh)

A week later, in mid-April, Payne was ready to rejoin the tour. The scene was Hilton Head, South Carolina, where he was trying to win his third straight MCI Heritage Classic. He came up short, tying for fourth, but it was still a very impressive return. Although he had sacrificed valuable ground to his competitors, there was still plenty of time to salvage the season, especially if he could somehow capture one of the three remaining majors. His first opportunity came in June in the U.S. Open at Hazeltine National Golf Club in Chaska, Minnesota. It was an opportunity he would not waste.

He opened with a five-under 67, tying Nolan Henke for the first-round lead. One would imagine that Payne would sleep pretty good after a start like that, but it was the exact opposite. That's because the mattress in his bed was too soft for his back. Payne quickly improvised, trading beds with his two-year-old son, Aaron. It must have worked. The next day, Payne shot a 70 to assume a one-stroke advantage. In two days, Payne had hit thirty-three of thirty-six greens in regulation, which, by Open standards—by any standards, actually—was an outstanding performance. Outstanding or not, there were still two more days to go, an eternity for any golfer, especially one not exactly known as a great closer.

Payne hung pretty tough on Saturday, recording a 73 to share the lead with Scott Simpson, the 1987 champion, heading into the final round. Simpson would be difficult to beat. He was the perfect Open player; he made few mistakes. For the first fifteen holes Sunday, he made very few. Payne, meanwhile, failed to capitalize on one birdie opportunity after another. As they reached the sixteenth tee, Payne was down by two. Another major was slipping away, and there seemed little he could do about it. Fortunately, his opponent did it for him. At sixteen, Simpson left a seven-iron approach in the high grass on his way to a bogey. Payne got his par to trail by just one. Then, after both players parred seventeen, Simpson came through with another bogey, setting up an eighteen-hole play-off for the following day. Payne had the momentum.

So much for momentum. Entering sixteen, in fact, Payne was in the exact predicament as he had faced the day before— trailing by two with only three holes to go. It seemed unlikely he could overcome that deficit two days in a row against a player with Simpson's patience and experience. Unlikely, not impossible. Payne birdied sixteen with a dramatic twenty-foot putt while Simpson bogeyed it by missing a three-footer. Suddenly, they were tied again. Simpson then bogeyed seventeen and eighteen, and it was over. For the week, he played the final three holes in eight over par; Payne in one under. That was the difference, as **Scott Simpson** *remembers:*

Payne hit some great shots the last few holes [of the play-off]. I thought I had him. But, to his credit, he never gave up. For a guy who had come in second as many times as he had, I thought he was pretty tough under the gun that week. We both had a really tough day [Payne shot 75; Simpson, 77]. It got windy, and the greens got really hard. It was pretty weird. Nobody was watching us—maybe a hundred people—while we were warming up on the range. Then, suddenly, when we got to the first tee, the whole fairway was lined with people.

—————

With so many split-second decisions to make, ABC producer **Terry Jastrow** *was usually too busy to display much emotion. But what he witnessed in the final holes at Hazeltine that Sunday forced him to make a rare exception:*

At the eighteenth hole, Payne hits his approach shot to the back left fringe. He's right up against the collar. At that moment, he pulls off the single bravest shot I have ever seen hit in a U.S. Open, and I was at every one of them starting in 1968. Keep in mind that it's the final hole of the final day of the U.S. Open, and he's tied and he's got about a thirty-footer that he's got to two-putt to make the play-off. He takes the toe of his putter, and though we've seen someone do this before, it takes an extraordinary amount of nerves to hit that shot in that situation. He does it. I couldn't believe it. I was out of my chair. It was outrageous that he would have enough guts to hit that shot and sure enough, he rolls it down to within several feet of the hole, and then knocks it in for his four and goes on to beat Scott Simpson the next day. I will never forget that putt and I thought it said a lot about him.

There was something else that said a lot about Payne—his performance in 1992. It said that he didn't respond too well to being the U.S. Open champion. As he later confessed, he felt he had to try a few new things to validate his new status and continue to improve. Unfortunately, he tried the wrong new things. He changed clubs and changed his swing, getting rid of the loop that had helped make him so successful. The result was that Payne finished forty-fourth on the money list, respectable by today's standards but his worst showing since his rookie season in 1981 when he made only ten starts.

The experiment was over. He went back to his old swing, and in 1993 he went back to his old results, again contending for the national championship, this time at Baltusrol Golf Club in Springfield, New Jersey. He was even tied for the lead on the back nine Sunday only to lose to Lee Janzen, who pulled a Tom Watson by chipping in from thirty feet at sixteen. Janzen had actually twice asked Payne, who was on the green forty feet away, if he preferred to play first, but Payne declined, waiting to see what his opponent would do. The strategy backfired. Who knows? If Payne had made his putt, Janzen might have felt added pressure and the chip might not have even come close.

*In any case, according to **Terry Jastrow**, if not for a bad break or two, Payne could have captured his second Open title in three years:*

He never really complained, but if there was ever a guy who had an abnormal amount of good luck, it was Lee Janzen at Baltusrol. On the tenth hole, Janzen hit his drive into the right rough. He was dead, Bob Rosburg-no-chance dead—capital *D*. He then played a very loose iron that went through a tree; it was blind luck. He knocks it up there on the green and makes par. Then, at the seventeenth hole, which is a par-five, you had to hit it in the fairway in order to get it over the stream in two. If you didn't, you were fighting with your life for a par. Janzen hit his tee shot straight right into a forest of trees but it careened out into the fairway from where he could then get it over the stream and make his par. Couple that with the nonsense with Janzen at the fifth hole at Olympic five years later, when the ball falls out of the tree as he's walking back to the tee, and Payne hitting it into the divot at twelve, and you're not going to find a guy, with the possible exception of Greg Norman, who was dealt worse cards by Lady Luck than was Payne Stewart, and yet he never complained. He was a gentleman about it.

---

*Jastrow wasn't the only one to admire how Payne handled his misfortune in 1993. So, too, was **Lee Janzen**, who barely knew him. Besides leaving that day with the U.S. Open trophy, he left with a lot of respect for his opponent:*

We hadn't really become friends yet. I think that was the first time I played with him. It was a very tense day for both of us. I think we were concentrating more on the golf than anything and not much on getting to know each other then. When it was over, he came over to me with a big smile on his face to congratulate me and tell me how my life was going to change. He was so genuinely happy for me, I was almost stunned. You reverse the position, I don't think I could be that happy for someone else. It was amazing. And then, hours later, I found bananas in my shoes. A couple of weeks earlier, he had [done the same thing] to Paul Azinger after he had holed a bunker shot [on the eighteenth hole] at Memorial [to beat Payne by a shot].[8]

In the years leading up to his proclaimed embracing of Christianity, Payne often found himself at a loss while his faith was being tested on the golf course. Here he is seeking answers during his disappointing loss to Lee Janzen in the 1993 U.S. Open at Baltusrol. (AP/Wide World Photos; Rusty Kennedy)

Not everyone applauded the way Payne acted at Baltusrol. Author **John Feinstein**, *who was just beginning his research on* A Good Walk Spoiled, *his best-seller about life on the PGA Tour, was especially turned off during one of Payne's appearances in the press tent:*

He was playing with John Daly the first two rounds, and Daly hit it on the par-five seventeenth in two, which nobody had ever done. Payne was two shots off the lead after the second round, so he was brought into the interview room. He went through his card and somewhere, fairly deep into the interview, Jayne Custred of the *Houston Chronicle*, who was six or seven months pregnant, asked him what he thought when he saw Daly knock it on at seventeen. Stewart just gave her this disdainful look and said, "I don't worry about what other players are doing. I worry about what Payne Stewart is doing." Actually, the first thing he said was, "Did he knock it on the green in two?" I thought, "What [a jerk]!" Obviously, he was aware that Daly had knocked it on in two. The crowd was whooping it up when he did it. All he had to do was say, "Wow, that's an amazing feat!" Obviously, somebody got to him because the next day, [on-course commentator] Mark Rolfing talked to him before the round and brought it up and he gave the right answer then. I remember rooting like [crazy] for Lee Janzen on Sunday even though I didn't know Lee Janzen from a hole in the wall.

———

Payne wouldn't get that close to a major championship in 1994. In fact, for the first time since 1984, he missed the cut in three of the four big ones; only a tie for sixty-sixth at the PGA spared him from total ineptitude. Overall, he finished 123rd on the money list with *only $145,687, even worse than his mediocre effort in 1992. The slump hit Payne pretty hard, as* **Jim Morris** *observed when they were paired together one year at Pebble Beach:*

After I came off the course, Payne and I had what I would call a father-and-son talk. He had had a pretty bad fit on that day. He had not conducted himself in a professional manner. I just asked if I could ride back with him from the course to the hotel. I didn't have to ask him any questions; he pretty much told me what had happened. I sat there, listened, and agreed with him. He needed someone with whom he could just air it out. First of all, after he missed his birdie putt and got a par, he picked up a coin on me. I had about a two-foot birdie putt, and it was on one of my [handicap] stroke holes. It was a mistake. He thought that was unprofessional of him. Then, for three or four holes, he was totally out of control. He hit a couple of bad shots, including one that he skulled out of the trap that hit a tree. Some gal ran off with his golf ball and he talked to her pretty strongly, and bent his wedge to where it looked kind of warped. He was just an unhappy camper. He was pushing too hard after the 1991 Open, and I think it affected everything he did. He had won the Open and now he had to prove he was worthy of being an Open champion. He wasn't at peace with himself.

—————

At peace or not, Payne did manage to win again. This time it was Scott Hoch who bailed him out. Hoch squandered a seven-shot lead in the final round of the 1995 Shell Houston Open, bogeying twelve, fourteen, and sixteen, and double-bogeying the seventeenth, where his ball found the lake fronting the green. Somehow Hoch *made a miraculous putt at eighteen to force a play-off, but all it did was postpone his agony. After it was over, **Hoch**, who had blown a great opportunity to win the 1989 Masters by missing a two-foot putt in a play-off with Nick Faldo, was despondent. He joked with the press about his last name rhyming with* choke. *Through it all, there was at least one moment he did appreciate:*

He said the right things to me. I've lost a few tournaments before and I've had people say the wrong things afterward. But Payne always knew the right thing to say. He had been on the other side and experienced defeat. He made me feel better. I couldn't have felt much worse at that point. I had let the tournament get away.[9]

A NEW PAYNE

I began to notice that there seemed to be a peace-fulness to him. He just suddenly, out of nowhere, talked about his new perspective on life. He became very emotional.

**—JIM NANTZ,
CBS GOLF HOST**

To some, maybe it was a smile. To others, maybe it was something he said. To almost everyone, it signified a big change, and one that was most welcome. Nobody can pinpoint the precise day the change began to occur, but there was no doubt that by the late-1990s, a new Payne Stewart had emerged. This one was less arrogant and more giving. So what was the source of this transformation? In 1999, Payne gave the answer—his faith in Jesus Christ. In June, at the U.S. Open at Pinehurst, Payne even wore a WWJD [What Would Jesus Do?] bracelet that his son, Aaron, had given to him, and he credited Jesus for his triumph. It was a side of Payne Stewart that many did not expect to see.

It is never easy to explain exactly what leads a person to embrace Jesus, and Payne was no exception. Some say it started years earlier when Paul Azinger, his best friend, was diagnosed with cancer. Others attribute it to the believers around him in Orlando, such as his agent, Robert Fraley, and his friend, major league baseball pitcher Orel Hershiser. And then there are those who give credit to Aaron and his older sister, Chelsea.

---

*Whatever the cause, one fact was irrefutable: There was a new Payne Stewart. CBS golf host **Jim Nantz** was at Pebble Beach in February 1999 when Payne went public with his beliefs. Nantz was surprised and moved by the whole scene:*

We had a suite on the ground floor of the Lodge, right off the eighteenth green, which we had made into our makeshift rain studio, and which is where we had the trophy presentation. I walked him through his history at Pebble Beach, having him explain how special it was for him to win the tournament. I began to notice that there seemed to be a peacefulness to him. He just suddenly, out of nowhere, talked about his new perspective on life. He became very emotional. In fact, he got so lost in the moment that it really shocked me. I felt a little blind-sided by it. He used to have that armor of protection up all the time, but it came tumbling down that day. I think that may have been the first time he showed that side of himself publicly. At one point, he paused, looked into the camera directly, and addressed Tracey and the kids, telling them how much he loved them. It was pretty powerful.

---

*It wasn't the first time that day that **Jim Nantz** had noticed a different Payne. Hours earlier, while hanging around the putting green, he recognized the change:*

As I always do, I was spending Sunday morning, casually saying hello to everybody. Payne was going through his warm-up exercises. He was extraordinarily gracious that day, more so, in fact, than I had ever seen him before, and I had had a lot of contact with him over the years, dating all the way back to his match against Fred Couples for the Southwest Conference Championship in 1979. Anyway, I noticed that he was putting with a new weapon. It had a red dot right above the face. He was making everything on the putting green, and I said, "Man, I've never seen you putt the ball so well." He reached his arm out and extended the putter to me. He says, "Here, try it. Here's what you do. Stand over the putt, and as soon as you completely cover the dot up with the shaft, that means your putter head is square. Then, you can't miss." So I tried it, and doggone, it worked! I just stroked them in. I'm always uncomfortable doing anything with a gallery out there. It's not my place, so I usually turn down those kind of offers. But something about that moment made me change my mind. He was so gracious.

———

*Payne's love for Jesus seemed to represent a dramatic shift in his spiritual views. **Scott Simpson** recalls a conversation they had once on their way back from the British Open:*

We were sitting on the Concorde and started talking about Christianity. He was kind of blowing me off. He didn't buy any of it. To see him come full circle in recent years and be wearing the bracelet was a pretty amazing thing.

Maybe it wasn't so amazing, after all. Because, as **Calvin Peete** *points out, Payne didn't come across as fulfilled as one might have expected for someone in his position. Peete, a senior tour professional who accompanied Payne to Morocco to participate in the annual Hassan II Trophy several years ago, recognized the signs:*

In his mannerisms, in his eyes, I could see that he wasn't happy with himself. He was happy, naturally, with his success on the tour, but not with himself. So it didn't surprise me at all when he started seeking Jesus Christ. I had seen the solitude in him, and the way he was searching for himself when we were in Morocco. That's what happens when you're drawn together in a foreign country. You get to know each other a little bit and even if you don't speak about these things, you can see what's going on in another person's life.

Larry Moody *also wasn't shocked by Payne's transformation. Moody, the longtime chaplain for the PGA Tour, had spent many hours over the years talking to him about how he related to God. Their lively and provocative conversations revealed a man in search of some answers:*

He had a lot of questions when his dad passed away [in 1985]. "Where did he go?" and "Why did God take my dad when he was so young?" We spent some time discussing all of that. That causes a lot of people to question how there could be a good God when that kind of suffering goes on. He came to eventually understand that we live in an unjust world, but God did not intend it to be that way. It was man's choice to disobey God that brought the pain and suffering that there is in the world. By 1991 Payne had won two majors and had buried the Avis title, but there wasn't a real sense of the longing peace that he had wanted. He thought it would come to him once he had achieved all of his success but it hadn't.

Then Payne started sending his kids to a Christian athletic camp in Branson, Missouri. While they were there, both children came to know what it meant to have a personal relationship with God through Christ. They would tell their dad about it, and he would listen. About the same time, Paul Azinger and Payne would go fishing after Paul's chemotherapy treatments. They would have these long talks. Paul was facing death while Payne had won two majors and a bunch of tournaments. Yet he saw a peace in Paul that he didn't have. They would talk about that. Paul had a phrase that I had given him when he was battling cancer in the initial stages, which stated, "We're not in the land of the living going to the land of the dying; we're in the land of the dying going to the land of the living." He shared that with Payne.

His agent, Robert Fraley, also had a tremendous influence on him. Robert had a very close relationship with God and would have numerous discussions with Payne. Payne would say, "Well, I know God and I believe Jesus was who he said he was." He never seemed to be at the point that some players I've talked to reach, where they're not even sure that there's a supreme being. But Payne still didn't have that personal relationship yet. Part of it was that he had a lot of trouble with hypocrites, people who claimed to be Christians but who he felt didn't walk the walk. So he wrestled with all of that. He didn't want to do something he couldn't follow through on.

Probably the one who had the biggest impact on him in the last two years was Orel Hershiser. They would play golf together. Orel had a Sunday school class at First Baptist Church. Payne went there and began to really understand even clearer what it meant to have that personal relationship with Christ. I knew for sure about a year and a half ago that Payne had that peace. He really got involved in personal Bible studies that last year. He had a little devotional he was reading through in the morning and evening. That gave him great encouragement.

When I saw him in April [at the Shell Houston Open], it was the first tournament he was wearing Aaron's WWJD bracelet. I teased him a bit, saying, "Payne, what's that on your wrist?" He said, "I'm making a big statement here." He told me Aaron had asked him to wear it. "You know, I'd come to the Bible study more," he said, "but I made so much fun of the hypocrites, people who came and then weren't perfect." I said, "Payne, the Bible study is for sinners only. The point at which you stop being a sinner, you can't come anymore. You'd make the rest of us feel bad." He thought that was a great perspective. He didn't want to be a Bible thumper. He wanted to show people that Jesus Christ had made a difference in his life. He was adamant that he wanted people to not just hear it come out of his mouth. He wanted them to see the changed life and that's why he was willing to wear the bracelet, to up the ante a little bit, to make sure he was living what he really felt in his heart.

The agony of defeat and Payne Stewart were companions throughout much of the 1980s, although the experiences that earned him the Avis label taught Payne how to be a comfort to others in pain. (AP/Wide World Photos; Dennis Gordon)

J. B. Collingsworth, *assistant pastor at the First Baptist Church in Orlando, enjoyed a front-row seat for Payne's growth as a Christian:*

I didn't see Payne as this worldwide figure. I wasn't enamored by who he was. I saw him as Payne Stewart, who happened to be a golfer but who was also my friend, and so I treated him that way. I think a lot of people embraced him and Tracey that way. I'm friends with a number of high-profile people, and once people like that know you are accepted, it helps them feel safe with you. He knew I was good friends with Orel Hershiser, so I think that made me safe. You have to approach a celebrity in a different way. I don't ever force myself on them. I try to love them where they are, and that's what I did with Payne.

In the beginning, it was real new to him. What happened was that he saw so many believers who were living out what they believed that it challenged him to really examine his own life. His children also began to challenge him. At our school, they would have to memorize Scripture. Parents help them with that, and I think that was a big part of what God used to teach Payne. He was surrounded at the school and church by Christian people who really cared about him. Payne just realized there was more to life than being successful. When you have everything that the world has to offer and you're not happy, you begin to look inside.

I went over with him how to be saved, giving him books to read. A year or so before he died, he began to read the Bible on a regular basis. He was real honest and a little awkward at first. He said, "I just don't know anything about the Bible." I said, "I can handle that." That's when I began to help him. He was eager to learn. I gave him a book, *Steps to Peace with God*, by Billy Graham. During that process of coming to Christ, he began to ask questions of other people. Once, when we had breakfast, I told him I had a class for him to attend. That next Sunday, he came and brought his family. Being on the road a lot, it was hard for him to be in church all the time. Sometimes, he would sneak in and not come to Bible study, which we have every Sunday. He would come to worship. When they found his belongings on the plane, they found four devotional books: One was *In His Grip*, by Wally Armstrong. Another was *A Handbook to Prayer* by Kenneth Boa, and there was also *A Handbook to Renewal* by the same author.

I went to his U.S. Open victory party at Isleworth Country Club on the Friday after the tournament. When I walked in, he held his hand up, pointed to his WWJD bracelet, and said, "It was him," and then he hugged us. We watched the last three holes together, and I noticed him just starting to tear up. He walked away to gather himself. He came back and was still crying. Afterward, I put my arm around him and I said, "I appreciate your heart," and he said, "J. B., I just want everybody to know it's Jesus. Jesus has done this. It's Jesus who has changed my life." The thing that I've thought about so many times since then is that everybody did know. People make snide remarks but unless you ever experience Christ, you don't understand, and he didn't understand for a long time. Once you do experience the peace, that's when you begin to realize that the power comes when we relinquish our own lives, our own wills, to God, the Father. He begins to remake us.

The sad part is that he was just beginning to learn and grow. There's no telling what he would have been as he grew older. I think the sky would have been the limit. Payne was reading the Book of John at the time of his death, and he told a friend that he was reading First Thessalonians a few weeks before. "Not even boring, really pretty good," he said, which was Payne's M.O. During that day at Isleworth, Dixie Fraley, Robert's wife, came up to me, put her finger in my chest, and said, "You need to disciple him, J. B. He loves you. You're the one." So just a week before he died, Payne and I talked about how we had to get going on the discipleship, which would have meant us talking about the Bible or Scripture, and what the Lord was doing in his life. It would have been challenging him to continue growing in his faith by reading and studying and delving into God's Word and not being afraid to ask questions. It didn't happen and that's my one regret.

But I feel that God had it all planned. Look at all the people who have come to know Christ as a result of his memorial service. Would that have happened otherwise? No. That plane veering off course and flying pilotless for four hours caught the attention of the world, allowing God to grip the hearts of people and then, through the service, God really gripped their hearts.

God mellowed Payne considerably and replaced all the bad with the good that comes from knowing the Lord. Payne told *Sports Illustrated* that there used to be a void in his life, and he didn't understand how he had lived so long without [his new peace]. He had a willingness to let God become first and foremost in his life. The Bible says Jesus came to save those who were lost. With someone who comes to know Christ later in life, when they realize the power of God in their lives as an adult, it just kind of blows them away, which is what happened with Payne. He was blown away.

—◄◄◄◦►►►—

*Like J. B. Collingsworth, **Pastor Jim Henry** of the First Baptist Church also witnessed a wonderful evolution in Payne's spirituality:*

When I met him the first time, which was before he came to Christ, I could tell that he was a little guarded. He was nice but I could tell that he didn't know what I was going to say or do. But once he came to know Christ, when we would begin to bump into each other at different times, there was a whole soft look on his face. He was so approachable. You could tell something was going on in his life that was good. One of the things that I'll always remember is when I went to our school's varsity football game. We were a little bit late and sat about ten rows behind Payne. I didn't even know he was there. Suddenly, I heard a bunch of guys singing "Happy Birthday" to me. I looked down and there was Payne, with his hat off, leading the song and waving at me. I couldn't imagine him doing that a few years ago, but I think he had come so far and felt so much at home spiritually with us. When he moved into the body of Christ, I think he felt, "Hey, I can kid this guy and sing; this guy's my brother."

A year ago, we had a celebrity golf tournament in which he gave a clinic. After the event was over, when my wife and I were walking back to our car, we saw Payne walking toward us. It was a cold day and raining off and on, but he stood and talked to us like we were old friends. He talked about our game, the school, and just how we were doing. He took time for us. He didn't try to hurry away. He could have thrown his clubs in the car and said, "Hey, good to see you, glad you had a good time," and left. To me, that was something special. He was treating me like the guys he played golf with.

What happened with Payne is not uncommon. Nearly every Sunday in our church, we'll have adult men and women come to Christ. We have a lot of people who get everything and they're still not satisfied. They realize there's got to be something else. I think part of it is that, living in a postmodern Christian society, a lot of people really hadn't heard that much about Jesus to know the difference he makes in one's life. In our culture, not as many people know *how* to come to Christ. When they find out, they know there's an emptiness in their lives and they're looking for him. Somebody said there are three questions a man has to answer: Why am I here? How did I get here? And where am I going? I think Payne had answered those questions.

—⟨⟩—

Shortly before he died, Payne donated $500,000 to the First Orlando Foundation to help pay for a new athletic complex for the First Academy, the school his children attended. **Randall James**, *president of the foundation, will never forget when he first received the incredible news:*

He called last September and said, "Make sure you bring the conceptual drawings of the complex, and, oh, by the way, I want you to know that Tracey and I are going to donate $500,000." I was just speechless. I knew he was going to give some money but I was thinking maybe $10,000 or $20,000, something like that. Never did I think it would be six digits. The first thing I could get out of my mouth was, "Thank you, Lord." We were very grateful. He invited about ten couples over to his house for a barbecue, and from those ten couples, there was an additional $800,000 that was given to our school. He did all the cooking and waited on folks. I was stunned. He put his money where his heart was. His daughter plays on our softball team. He wanted all of the kids at the First Academy to have a first-class athletic complex.

He was very active in the Bible study at our church. Payne was growing in the Word. Now, was he a mature Christian? No, not yet. In fact, in my humble opinion, none of us will be mature Christians until we go to heaven. But there was a definite trend in his spiritual growth. A week before he was killed, I had a First Orlando Foundation annual banquet to raise money for our center for pregnancy. That was when we gave Payne our annual Legacy Award. The theme of the event was: Life is precious. The proceeds went to our center. Payne was not as knowledgeable about the center, but he was very interested in hearing more about it. So I shared with him what our counselors do. Then we had three young women come up and give testimonies of how they came to our center to get an abortion. One out of every five people who come here or call our center think it's an abortion clinic. Instead of just telling them we're not one, we tell them to come in to talk to us. We share the Gospel and the sanctity of life. These three women received Christ into their hearts and decided to have their babies. They just wanted to thank the women at the center, the counselors, for sharing with them the truth of God's Word.

When they got up and gave their testimonies, I was sitting at the table next to Payne. There were tears rolling down his cheek. It had quite an impact. When the program was over, instead of standing around and shaking hands with everybody who was congratulating him, he made a beeline straight over to that table to tell those three young women that they were the ones who should have been honored instead of him. Those kinds of things tell me that Christ really ruled in his heart.

I shared a Scripture with him last June or July that I was proud of his being obedient to Proverbs, where it states, "In all your ways, acknowledge him and he will direct your paths." I said, "Payne, that's what you're doing now. You're acknowledging Christ as the giver of your success and he'll continue to lead you," and he did, up until the time he took him home. He just had a big smile and said, "Yep." He was always concerned about the school and what we could do to make it better. He talked to me after the shooting at Columbine. "We've been pretty blessed," he said. "Nothing like that has happened here, but we want to make sure we're doing all we can do." I told him we were looking at other measures to enhance the safety of our kids.

The Payne who cried that night in Orlando might have been unrecognizable to those who hung out with him in the 1980s and early 1990s. Golf writer **Greg Stoda**, *who saw the best and worst in Payne, believes the transformation began when Paul Azinger was diagnosed with cancer:*

Payne just grew up. There's nothing sexy about that, but that's what happened. Before, there was this sense, "I'm young and strong and rich and nothing is ever going to hurt me." Then, maybe his best friend in the entire world comes down with cancer, and he's very shaken by that, especially with the fact that he had also lost his father at a relatively young age [Bill Stewart was sixty-four] from cancer. During Paul's most difficult time, Payne was one of the constants, one of the guys who was always there beyond the cursory phone calls. Payne probably doesn't deserve any huge credit for that. He was a really good friend and that's what really good friends should be doing. But the fact that he was so supportive might have helped Payne as much as it helped Paul come to grips with what was going on. Somewhere along the line, a light bulb went on in Payne's head. He realized this wasn't the way he wanted to live his life.

———

However it evolved, Payne's new commitment to his religion sent a powerful message. One person profoundly affected was LPGA Hall of Famer **Carol Mann**, *who decided to more closely examine her own feelings toward God:*

I thought I was a good person who did good things and had a good relationship with God, but it was more a case of when I needed him. I had also always sensed a barrier between me and what I call the "God Squad" on the PGA Tour—guys like Scott Simpson and Larry Mize, who started talking about God when they won majors in the late 1980s. I was thinking these guys didn't have the best sense of PR because the press wasn't going to write about this stuff. So I was critical during those days. But when I saw what Payne said about how he felt he walked with Jesus during the final round of the Open, I was stunned and incredibly touched. I had no idea the depth of Payne's spirituality and his relationship with God. As a result, Payne Stewart, in his death, has reached out to me to the point that I began to question my own relationship with God, and I have now started a course of action to establish a whole different relationship. I've started to read books. One is called *The Plan of God*. The material is just staggeringly important. Every moment has a cumulative effect on me. This might be his most important legacy. When I say a swear word, I feel guilty now. I never felt guilty about that. When I take a cigarette, I feel guilty. I'm just at the beginning.

—⚙⚙⚙—

The change in Payne took on many forms, and they weren't always very dramatic. For **Larry Rinker**, *who had known him since they both joined the tour in the early 1980s, one conversation was very telling:*

I noticed it in 1997, when I was playing the tournament in Las Vegas. I was 125th on the money list [and was trying to earn his card for the following year]. Well, I ended up making the cut [and getting his card]. He was one of the guys who called to congratulate me and we wound up back at the Mirage Hotel. He then started asking me about the round. Before, he would have been more into his own thing.

—⚙⚙⚙—

For **Chip Beck**, *another veteran tour player, it was the way Payne greeted him one day that stood out:*

He was always pretty tough with me, calling me Charles while everyone else calls me Chip, especially the people who know me, and he certainly knew me, playing on three Ryder Cups [1989, 1991, 1993] together. But in the last year, he was a different person. The Wednesday before he died, my wife saw him coming up to me at the

Disney tournament. "Hey, Chipper, how you doing?" he said. He never called me "Chipper." She later said that she almost fell out of the cart as she watched that. She told me she had never seen him act that nice to me.

Payne got to share some time with Ohio teenager Joel Broering as part of A Special Wish Foundation. Broering later passed away from leukemia, but not before Payne had given the youngster his trophy from the 1993 Skins Game. (Paul Lester Photography)

OLYMPIC AND PINEHURST

He had a lot less game when he won his second Open. . . . How was he doing this? [The answer]— absolute guts, and that you don't have to be the best all the time to win. You just have to pick your spots, and I think he had figured that out.

**—MARK LYE,
FRIEND AND TV GOLF COMMENTATOR**

In June 1998 the son attempted to succeed where the father had come up short. Forty-three years earlier, Missouri amateur Bill Stewart had competed in the U.S. Open at the Olympic Club in San Francisco, the year that Jack Fleck went on to register his remarkable upset over the great Ben Hogan. Unfortunately, Bill Stewart didn't come close to making that kind of an impression, recording two very forgettable rounds—83 and 88. The traveling salesman would have to hit the road again. Eventually, the son learned all about the father's history at Olympic. More importantly, he learned how much the national championship had meant to him. So much, in fact, that when Payne first became eligible to play in the Open, Bill Stewart insisted that his son write his full name, "William Payne Stewart" on the entry form. Which, of course, is what the obedient son did.

Payne got off to an excellent start at Olympic in the '98 Open, shooting a four-under 66 to take a two-stroke lead over Bob Tway and Tom Lehman. For Payne, it was the fourth time in nine years that he had been atop the U.S. Open leader board after eighteen holes. On Friday, he stayed on top with a 71, although an incident on the eighteenth green provided an omen that, despite his outstanding play, it might not be his week. He three-putted from ten feet, and it wasn't his fault. The USGA was the culprit for placing the pin in an almost impossible location. At worst, Payne should have faced a three- or four-footer for par. Instead, his initial birdie putt trickled all the way down the hill, leaving him about twenty feet away. He bogeyed the hole.

That was only the beginning of his troubles. On Sunday, Payne, who enjoyed a four-stroke advantage entering the day and seemed a good bet to join Ernie Els as the only players with two Open wins in the 1990s, began to falter just as Lee Janzen, his nemesis from Baltusrol, began to climb up the leader board. The tournament had really tightened up by the time Payne teed off on twelve. His drive was in the fairway. He was in good shape. Or was he? When he got to his ball, he discovered that it had come to rest in a sand-filled divot. He was upset, of course, but there was nothing he could do about it. According to the rules, a sand-filled divot is not considered ground under repair. Payne proceeded to bogey the hole. Soon afterward, to make matters worse, USGA official Tom Meeks told Payne and playing partner Tom Lehman that they had been put on the clock. One more bad time, and they would each receive a one-stroke penalty.

Ultimately, when Payne lost the tournament—his last courageous bid for a birdie at eighteen turned away just before reaching the hole—many familiar with his record expected he might pout and point blame. He didn't. Instead, he showed class. CBS commentator **Peter Kostis** *was one of many who noticed the difference:*

I knew that he had grown up as a person and a player when I saw how he reacted to his ball landing in the divot. The old Payne Stewart would have thrown a temper tantrum. He would have bemoaned the fact that after grinding his butt off for some sixty-five holes, how in the world could this happen to him? But he looked at his ball and kind of snickered and laughed. The expression on his face was one of resignation. He kept chewing his gum. It was like, "If this is what the Lord has in store for me, then I got to do the best I can."

———

A few minutes after signing his scorecard, Payne was interviewed by NBC's **Roger Maltbie**. *Stunned by how he had let another major championship slip away, Payne now had a great opportunity in front of a national audience to air his frustration about the sand-filled divot or the time warning. But, as Maltbie remembers, his old friend chose the high road:*

The style and the grace in the way he handled that defeat and the interview he did with me was really kind of an awakening for me. In 1989, when Mike Reid faltered down the stretch at Kemper Lakes, Payne wasn't particularly gracious in his victory and he was noted for that. When he was younger, there were people he rubbed the wrong way. He was pretty much convinced that nobody was as good as he was. I think there was a side of him that felt that when somebody else beat him, they got lucky. But that all seemed different in 1998. At Olympic, he was effusive in his praise of Lee Janzen. He was more than gracious.

———

*In the booth, Maltbie's colleague, analyst **Johnny Miller**, was just as impressed with Payne's demeanor:*

That was a tough thing for him to take, but he was such a pro at that point. The only other comparison in modern day was the way Greg Norman took it when he lost to Nick Faldo at the Masters in 1996. They both showed a lot of dignity in defeat. A lot of players would have taken a totally different approach to that loss at Olympic. He took it like a man, and obviously it didn't destroy him enough so that he wasn't able to win at Pinehurst the next year. What happened to him at Olympic was the perfect Hollywood setup to him winning at Pinehurst. He had the U.S. Open kind of game with his beautiful tempo and played within himself and was a great ballstriker. He hit the ball high and soft, which was perfect for Open courses. He obviously knew how to handle the tough things that happen at a U.S. Open because he had a lot of good chances.

———

*Back home, in Springfield, **Jim Morris** was heartbroken. But while watching his great friend cope so well with the disappointment, he came to another realization, which he later shared with Payne:*

Because of the way he handled himself, I told him that his dad would have been more proud of him right then than with any triumph he might have had. He would have known that Payne had busted his butt, doing the absolute best job he could, and that the other guy just happened to get a break or two and beat him. That's the way Bill Stewart was. He was as great a loser as he was a winner. He was so competitive, but if you beat him, he would be the first guy to seriously congratulate you.

Payne is flanked by longtime friend Jim Morris and Bill Stewart, Payne's dad, back home in Missouri. (Photo courtesy of Jim Morris)

After doing the Maltbie interview, Payne proceeded to do a taped interview with ESPN's Karl Ravech. He had just started, when **Craig Smith***, manager of media relations for the USGA, interrupted him. Smith dreaded what he was about to say. But, thanks to Payne, the uneasiness didn't linger:*

We always ask the runner-up to be part of the prize ceremony, which I think is very tough. I never ask the runner-up to go to the green, except for that part. Anyway, I went up to him when he was doing the interview with Ravech, and I said, "Payne, they're going to get to this part in two minutes. I really have to get you down there." He finished his answer to Karl's question, winked, and said, "Come on, let's go." Here's a guy who had just lost the U.S. Open, yet he's running down the hill at Olympic to get to the green in time for the ceremony. The way he had composed himself within ten minutes was simply incredible.

Payne's ordeal was only beginning. He knew the press would have some good questions, and he wouldn't be able to get away without giving some good answers. Surprisingly, the session with several hundred members of the Fourth Estate came off better than many might have expected. Golf writer **Melanie Hauser** *summarizes:*

To have two losses to Lee Janzen and have a roomful of people sitting there, pointing, "Lee Janzen got you again," that could not have been the easiest thing to do. Everybody had thought Payne was going to win this thing, and he didn't. But he handled it very, very well. I'll always remember him winking and saying, "I will be back." With that, he walked off the stage, put his arm around his mom, and said, "Come on, Mom, let's go." You believed it. It wasn't the cocky kid from 1989; it was a guy who was confident in his game, who truly believed that, next time, it was going to be his turn.

—⬗—

*Maybe so, but next time would still be a whole year away. Until then, he would have to live with the disappointment, knowing how close he had come to his third major championship, and, at age forty-one, perhaps aware he might never get that close again. Yet, on the very day after his Olympic loss, Payne proved he would be just fine. He played in an outing halfway across the country, in Quincy, Illinois, that would raise money for youngsters with special needs. To the amazement of fellow tour player **Charlie Rymer**, Payne was in a cheerful mood:*

It was incredible how Payne acted. Most people, on the day after losing a major championship the way he did, would have been really down, kind of grumpy. But he was so upbeat, it was unbelievable. We had a lot of fun at the auction that day. In fact, he donated the knickers that he had worn the day before. I remember looking at them and saying, "Payne, these are kind of soiled," and I never heard him laugh so hard. He didn't have much of a comeback for that one. Later that same day, he and I were on a plane together. He started asking me what I was doing in my career. I told him I was playing the Nike Tour but wasn't enjoying myself. He then came down hard on me, telling me I needed to have more confidence in myself.

Here's a guy whom I didn't know that well, and he was taking the time and really trying to help me.

———

*One person who was not surprised by how Payne dealt with Olympic was good friend **Todd Awe**. For years, Awe had seen Payne learn from defeat, and this time was no different:*

With a lot of people, it could have devastated their career. They would never have been able to come back. Payne didn't look at it that way. It gave him a new resolve that he could be competitive enough to win an Open, so that's what he dedicated himself to do. He said, "Hey, it's one shot. If I can get that far, that's 99.9 percent of the way there. That proves to me that I can get over the hill, and next year, I'm going to." He used it as a motivation, which he had done throughout his career. Whether it was [failing to qualify at the tour school] and going to Asia or whether it was losing the Byron Nelson [in 1985], he always had that kind of resolve that people couldn't believe. With all the times this guy finished second, didn't it drive him crazy? The answer was no. It proved to him that he was good enough, and that at some point, it was going to be his day. He was never discouraged. I remember after the Nelson tournament [which he blew with two straight double bogeys], we went over to some friends' house. We had dinner, laughed it up, and looked at that big check [$54,000] that Payne got. It was not a singing-the-blues-type situation. It was, guess what, he's playing next week at Colonial! We probably felt worse about the loss than he did, because he knew he was going to be put in that position again.

Like Greg Norman in 1996, Payne may have attracted more new supporters in defeat than in victory. One was author **John Feinstein**, *who was working on* The Majors, *his best-selling account of golf's four biggest tournaments in 1998. Feinstein, who had rooted against Payne five years earlier at Baltusrol, encountered a much different man this time around:*

When he handled everything so well after losing to Janzen, I knew I had to get a long session with him because he and Lee were the story on the last day of the Open. So we eventually got together two months later at the PGA in Seattle, at [NFL defensive tackle] Cortez Kennedy's house; Kennedy was represented by Robert Fraley, too. Payne cooked steaks on the outdoor grill, and then he and I went and sat on the patio in the back. We talked with the tape recorder running for about three hours. Then, when I shut it off, we started talking about his dad and my mom because my mom had died very suddenly a few years earlier. We talked about how much he missed him, even years later, and how certain things make you think about them constantly. He got emotional on several occasions. The most emotional was when he talked about the fact that, as important as it was for him to win the majors, a part of him felt gypped because his dad wasn't there to see him get to that level. Therefore, the win he would always enjoy the most would be Quad Cities [in 1982] because that's the one [victory] his father attended.

What really hit me that night was that it had been so important to Payne to handle losing because it was something he had not done well in the past. He said that as soon as he missed that last putt, he sort of had a talk with himself, "You've got to go through this for the next hour. You've got to answer the questions and not do what you've done in the past. Not be snappish." And he did it. He told me he handled Kemper Lakes very badly. He used the word *immature*. Looking back on it, he said, the first mistake he made was sticking around the scorer's tent. He should've gotten out of there and gone to the practice tee to hit balls in case there was a play-off, or he should have gone back into the clubhouse. Staying there and mugging for the camera and showing off his logos was immature. He said he wasn't dancing on Mike Reid's grave, but he could see where people might have gotten that impression. He also said that he thought that because he behaved that way, the media didn't want to give him credit for shooting a 31 on the back nine. They wanted to say that Mike Reid gave the tournament away. That really bothered him, which was why winning the Open in '91 was that much more important to him because he felt people couldn't say he backed into that one.

He's one of the few athletes I've ever met who, right in the middle of his career, at a time when he was a rich and famous person, looked himself in the mirror and said, "Hey, there are times when I'm [a jerk]." Usually what happens is that when they quit and aren't having their [back side] kissed anymore, they want people to pay attention to them, so they become good guys. It's the old cliché of wanting to say hello when it's time to say goodbye. Payne was trying to say hello when it was still time to say hello.

He told me this story about the Masters in 1996 when he and Tracey were walking out of the clubhouse. He had missed the cut. Some guy came up and asked him for an autograph, and Payne said, "No, I'm not allowed [in that particular area] to sign autographs." The guy said he wanted it for his little boy, and, according to Payne, he whirled on him, "Get away from me. I told you I can't sign." He looked at Tracey and Tracey had this horrified look on her face, like, How could you treat the poor man this way? He said he embarrassed her. Tracey ended up apologizing to the guy. Payne said at that point he went back to Robert Fraley who, at times, had encouraged him to do some media training. I think he went to Houston for three days. Payne was bright enough to understand that he did have this side to him. He had been incorrect that day at the Masters. He could sign autographs. Later, when he got in the car, it hit him that the guy was right. He realized he really was [a jerk].

The relationship between Payne and **Tom Meeks**, *director of rules and competitions for the USGA, didn't get off to a good start. Meeks, after all, was the official who had given Payne a bad time in the final round at Olympic. Eventually, though, the two became friends:*

The following spring, I was down at Isleworth in Orlando to do a workshop when I saw Payne on the range. He said, "You and I got to talk." We made plans to get together. When I got [to Isleworth], one of the assistant pros said, "Payne just called. He's running a little late but he said to get your shoes on, get your clubs, because when he gets here, the two of you are going to go out and play." Which is what we did— Payne, his son Aaron, and myself. It was wonderful to see him and his son together. When Aaron got a little discouraged, Payne told him to keep his confidence.

Meanwhile, Payne and I talked about things like the USGA's pace of play and sand-filled divots. I told him I didn't see any point in the future where the USGA would make the divots ground under repair. I then asked him a question: "Have you ever practiced any shots out of sand-filled divots?" He looked at me and said, "No," and I said, "Why not? You could do it here at Isleworth." He looked at me and said, "You're impossible." He had a little smirk because he knew that I had got him, that I had a better answer than he did. When Payne had won at Hazeltine in 1991, he didn't know anyone from the USGA and nobody knew him. Why? I think it was because he didn't want to be close to anybody on our side. I don't know if he was afraid of us or just wanted to keep that distance. But I got to know him last year and discovered he was a neat guy.

—————

*That's something **John Goldstein** already knew. Goldstein, who conducts off-camera interviews for NBC's golf coverage, did a one-on-one with Payne in October 1998 for the network's annual show reviewing the year's USGA championships. He soon found out that Payne's assessment of Olympic was still upbeat:*

Not only was he happy to sit down, but he gave so much of his time. We had some technical and lighting problems in the room they gave us, yet he was totally patient. Then, when the cameras started to roll, he went over a painful week in exquisite detail. Everything about the week he saw as a positive for the future. This wasn't just the stiff upper-lip stuff he gave people on the green with Lee Janzen or in the pressroom later that afternoon or even the following week when it was still a hot story. This was four months later.

———⌗———

In June 1999 "next time" was finally here. The site was North Carolina's Pinehurst No. 2, a masterpiece crafted by one of the game's legendary golf architects, Scotland native Donald Ross. Known for its difficult crowned greens, the course promised to provide a U.S. Open that emphasized the short game more than ever. Many approaches would slide helplessly off the putting surface, requiring the best players in the world to constantly demonstrate the kind of boldness and creativity they don't normally exhibit the rest of the year.

Payne was prepared for the assignment. For one thing, he possessed an excellent short game; for another, for the first time in several years, he was playing superb golf. His victory earlier in the season at Pebble Beach, his first since the Shell Houston Open in 1995, had been followed by outstanding performances at the Honda Classic [second, two shots behind Vijay Singh] and the MCI Classic [a tie for second, losing in a play-off to Glen Day]. And although he missed the cut a week before the Open, at the FedEx St. Jude Classic in Memphis, there seemed little doubt that, with a national championship at stake, he would elevate his game once again.

***Jimmy Roberts** certainly believed that to be the case. Roberts, who reports on golf for ESPN and ABC, arrived in Pinehurst early enough to join Payne and Scott Hoch for a practice round on Sunday. A few days later, as a guest on a syndicated radio show, Roberts picked Payne to win the tournament:*

I always try to get to the site of a major championship, if I'm not familiar with the course, on the Sunday before the event begins because what I always find is that there are players who want to avoid the rush and get a practice round in without any fans around. I've always been able to find someone I know well enough that I can ask if I can walk with them inside the ropes during the practice round. There's no security yet, so nobody really cares. I joined Payne and Scott on the second or third hole that day. Chuck Cook was there, too. I had the most wonderful guided tour of Pinehurst that a journalist could ever have in preparing for a week at the Open. Payne showed me what he was trying to do, what the problems were that might lie ahead and how to attack them. It was tremendous. This was his day at the office, yet he would hit a shot and walk over to me and say, "This is what you've got to look for here." He was very, very giving.

One of the specifics that came out of the day was how many different clubs a player could end up using if he were just off the green. The big issue that week was about how the greens were so crowned. At the fifteenth green, I believe, we stepped aside while he hit the same shot with four different clubs, and I thought that was really neat. The thing that stuck with me most was his attitude that day. Though he had played badly and missed the cut the week before, he was feeling great. I remember thinking to myself, "Now, that's odd. The guy just missed the cut." But he was so completely confident. He was stinging the ball, just hitting it so well.

Scott Hoch was equally impressed with Payne during the practice round, especially with the way he and swing coach Chuck Cook prepared so efficiently:

They were so meticulous. They mapped out everything. That was probably the best thing that could have happened—that he played poorly in Memphis and got there [to Pinehurst] early. They charted everything: where they wanted to hit it, if he missed it. And I imagine they had a few spots they had Xs on, where no matter what you do, you can't miss it there. I was more or less trying to get a feel for the course instead of mapping everything out the first day. And they started the first day and were doing it even the second day. So I guess by the third or fourth, they had it pretty much down. . . . At a U.S. Open-type course, it takes patience, and he had plenty of it. I think he knew that other people would not have it.[10]

———

The extra effort paid huge dividends. In Thursday's opening round, Payne recorded a two-under 68 to trail the leaders by a shot. On Friday, he made up that difference, sharing the top spot with David Duval and Phil Mickelson. Payne took the lead by himself after the third round—by one over Mickelson and two over Tiger Woods and Tim Herron, again putting himself in a final group on Sunday in the final round of a U.S. Open. Only one question remained—a big one: Could Payne Stewart hold the lead this time? NBC golf producer Tommy Roy didn't have an answer, though he came away with a lasting memory when he stopped at the driving range Saturday evening:

There were only two players left as darkness was rapidly approaching—Payne Stewart and Tiger Woods. But while Tiger had his whole big entourage of maybe thirty people watching him, Payne was at the other end all by himself, banging balls. Not even his caddie, Mike Hicks, was there. I remember that he had such a purposeful look on his face. That particular image really stands out for me, more so than all the great replays we had of him after he won the tournament.

⸺✦⸺

The purposeful face remained intact on Sunday, though late in the round, it appeared that it might not be enough. After bogeying the fifteenth, where he missed an eight-footer, Payne was one behind Mickelson, who possessed the kind of short game that could handle Pinehurst's nuances even more skillfully than Payne could. If that wasn't disarming enough, Tiger Woods was also within range. Perhaps it was the urgency of the situation that forced Payne to be too aggressive with his chip at sixteen, as he sent it twenty-five feet past the pin. Now he was in real danger. Somehow he maintained his composure and made the putt. And then, when Mickelson promptly bogeyed, Payne was suddenly tied for the lead again. With new life, he hit a beautiful six-iron to within three feet at seventeen, and made the putt to take the lead again by himself. Only one hole remained between him and his second U.S. Open title.

He wasn't going to make it easy. His drive landed in the rough, forcing him to lay up about eighty yards in front of the green. Getting up and down with so much at stake did not seem very likely; a Monday play-off with Mickelson did. But Payne couldn't wait for another day. This was his day. He knocked his approach to within fifteen feet, leaving himself a pretty straight putt, which he eventually made to win. Payne hugged Hicks and consoled Mickelson. It was an amazing finish. Television analyst and 1973 U.S. Open champion **Johnny Miller** *looks back:*

The way he made those putts the last three holes, nobody had ever done that before. He made three putts that made anyone else's performance over the last three holes look pretty dull. The putt he made at sixteen was a near-impossible putt over the hill and down the hill into the hole. And then he hits that drive in the right rough at eighteen, has a bad lie, but has enough Moxie to say, "Hey, this lie stinks. I'm going to just lay it up and put the ball underneath the hole and take my chances." That's just what he did. Nobody makes that putt at eighteen. The fact is that it's the hardest putt in golf to make—straight uphill with no break. You push it, it misses right. You pull it, it misses left. Most people leave it short, and if they do hit it hard enough, they usually pull it. For him to make that putt after making the two putts the holes before and winning the way he did, if he hadn't died until he was ninety, it [still] would have been historic. The minute he made that putt at the Open, I'm thinking, "This guy has won three majors. I'm going to vote for him to go in the Hall of Fame." Forget the fact that he passed away. His record, with his consistency and the three majors, I would vote for him to go in the Hall of Fame unemotionally. Even if he didn't win a lot of tournaments and a lot of people do remember him as Avis in the early years, he made a lot of good improvements in his life, and that's what we're down here for, to improve ourselves.

―⸺⸺―

Many people were happy for Payne, including two-time U.S. Open winner **Andy North***, who covered the tournament for ESPN:*

Payne and I had played many practice rounds at the Open over the years. He was great around the greens, and one of the reasons he was so good was that he loved to watch other people and try to learn from them. That was the essence of what we were doing. He understood early in his career that this was a championship he could win. His short game was terrific, he had a good head on his shoulders, and he had great patience. After he won, he was going to do a [taped] sit-down with Jimmy Roberts once we were finally off the air. I went down and met him in the hallway. We just looked at each other and gave each other a big hug. Not a single word needed to be said. Both of us had tears rolling down our cheeks.

—⊸▥▥▥⊷—

Payne got a lot of hugs that evening, including one from the USGA's **Tom Meeks**. *A year earlier, at Olympic, Meeks had given him a warning for slow play. This time, all he could give him was praise:*

After Saturday's play, I arrived at the range ready to talk to the Golf Channel. Payne's there, too, hitting balls. Just as he sees me, he turns to his caddie, "Mike, give me some balls for these sand-filled divots. Here comes Tom Meeks." He had told me after either Thursday's or Friday's round that he had been in three sand-filled divots and had made birdie, par, and bogey. "Well, you're getting better," I told him. Then I saw him a little while later on the putting green and he asked: "How fast do you want me to play tomorrow?" I said, "Payne, I want you to finish at ten till seven." He laughed and finished on Sunday at twelve to seven.

Watching him play those last nine holes, you had to look at his eyes. Or how he chewed that gum. The only other person that ever made more of an impression on me chewing gum was Rod Steiger in *In the Heat of the Night*. He was chewing his gum like it was part of what he had to do to stay focused. I was in my cart by the eighteenth green when he made the putt on Sunday. About ten minutes later, I went by the scoring area and just as I got down there, he walked out and saw me. He grabbed me, took me into the doors of the tunnel that goes into the locker room, and gave me a huge hug. He said, "Tom Meeks, you set up one heck of a golf course." That was as emotional a thing as I've ever had.

Guess who has just made the winning putt at the 1999 U.S. Open at Pinehurst. (AP/Wide World Photos; Chuck Burton)

—◄◄▸▸—

*How did Payne win the Open? It was a good question, and one
that many people asked, including his longtime friend and fellow
band member, **Mark Lye**. Lye spent the week reporting on the
tournament for the Golf Channel. Ultimately, he came up with one
explanation for why Payne had prevailed:*

He had a lot less game when he won his second Open. If
you go over the stats [so far that year], and we even said it
on the set at Pinehurst, he was something like 140th in
greens in regulation and 125th in fairways hit. How was
he doing this? [The answer]—absolute guts, and that you
don't have to be the best all the time to win. You just have
to pick your spots and I think he had figured that out.

—◄◄▸▸—

*If guts did make the difference, it meant Payne had come a long
way since his Avis days. **Jaime Diaz**, who writes about the PGA
Tour for Sports Illustrated, was on hand for much of the progres-
sion. At Pinehurst, he was as surprised as anyone:*

I really never thought of Payne as tough, which is why
Pinehurst was so inspiring to people. I think before that
they saw him as a vulnerable guy, not a tough guy, and yet
he was the toughest guy that day. That was the transformation that made him so appealing. Of all the people,
you didn't figure he would be the one to do what he did
on eighteen, to make maybe the biggest putt in the history of the U.S. Open. It was almost like an Everyman
conquest. Most of us choke and can't handle the pressure,
so people had identified with Payne in that regard. He

was a guy who had blown a lot of tournaments, and, at Pinehurst, he overcame all of that. I couldn't believe that it was him. I could see Tiger doing it or Janzen or Mickelson. But not Payne. How did he get so mentally tough? Well, I think the religious thing could be a part of it. Because, before that, he was clearly a guy who had lacked a meaningful internal life. I think his weakness under pressure was a manifestation of that. Then, he embraces God and he seems so much more mentally together.

⚬⚬⚬

Byron Nelson, one of Payne's biggest supporters, was watching the championship from his ranch in Roanoke, Texas. Nelson, eighty-eight, has seen a lot of great champions over the years. What he observed at Pinehurst that day should put Payne on that list:

When I was an announcer for ABC, I could tell a lot of times when Arnold was going to win or when Jack was going to win, just by their attitude, how they walked and acted, the expression on their faces. They were completely focused on what they were doing. Payne did that better at the Open in 1999 than I had ever seen him. Even when he got ready to hit that putt on the last hole, I said, "I think he's going to make it. I really do." I talked to Tracey about it later, and she agreed. He was so determined after what had happened the year before when he kind of threw the tournament away. He was really charged up for the Open last year, like Nicklaus used to be and Hogan used to be. You get a different type of expression in your face. You're not unpleasant but you look like nothing is bothering you. Peggy [Nelson's wife] and I called after he had won, and I told him I had never seen him that focused, and he said, "I felt that way all through the tournament. I had no trouble concentrating and if I missed a shot, it didn't bother me." He was as happy as he could be and I don't think I was ever any happier about anyone winning a tournament than I was to see him win.

—⁂—

*By winning his second U.S. Open in such in a courageous manner at the age of forty-two, Payne had more than made up for Olympic. He had made up for every near miss from his past. He also once again displayed the new maturity that had been sorely lacking in his younger years. The USGA's **Craig Smith** recalls an example that took place long after most people had left Pinehurst that night:*

The national Fox station out of Los Angeles had been hounding me all week to get one-on-ones with the players. That could be an endless parade, so we try and group everybody together as much as we can, except for the contracted networks. Come Sunday night, I was trying to get Payne out of the press tent at a reasonable hour so he could enjoy his victory. Yet the Fox people were hovering around the clubhouse, now trying to get a one-on-one with Payne. I said, "No, it's impossible. It's not going to happen." I guess Payne overheard me because he just stopped and said, "Can I help? What do you need?" And this was a guy who had just been put through the ringer for two hours. "Sure, we can do that," he said. He was an uncommon champion.

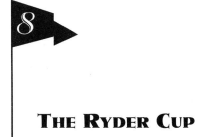

THE RYDER CUP

He had built his whole game around making the Ryder Cup these last two years, and yet he was willing to admit right there that he didn't feel like he was capable of helping the team. . . . I also remember the tears he had in his eyes as he spoke to the team Saturday night.

—**BRUCE LIETZKE,
ASSISTANT TO U.S. RYDER CUP CAPTAIN
BEN CRENSHAW, 1999**

———

It was hard to tell what excited Payne more about Pinehurst—winning another major or earning a trip to The Country Club in Brookline, Massachusetts, site of the 1999 Ryder Cup matches. Payne, after all, had been saying for months that competing again for his country in the Ryder Cup was a top priority. At forty-two, he knew he would not have many chances left. He had already wasted two of them—in 1995 at Oak Hill and 1997 at Valderrama—by not playing well enough to qualify on points, or to be selected as a captain's pick. The only way he would represent Uncle Sam again was to earn it himself, and now he had done just that. Along with Tom Lehman and perhaps Hal Sutton, Payne would be one of the team leaders, a role he coveted, an apprenticeship of sorts for the day when he hoped he would be in charge. He couldn't wait for Brookline. He had felt so powerless while watching the U.S. come up short at Oak Hill and Valderrama, especially since he believed his fiery presence could have made a difference. Now he would have a chance to prove it.

Payne made his first Ryder Cup squad in 1987 when the teams met at the Jack Nicklaus-designed Muirfield Village Golf Club in Dublin, Ohio. There was a lot at stake for the Americans, who were seeking revenge against a European unit that had been victorious two years earlier for the first time since 1957. A second straight defeat would be devastating. Losing in Europe was one thing; losing on American soil would be quite another. But that's exactly what happened, as the Europeans, led by perhaps the most intense competitor in the world, Seve Ballesteros, as well as the likes of Bernhard Langer and Ian Woosnam, outdueled the United States, 15–13.

———————

For his part, Payne won one out of three matches in the foursomes and four-balls, and beat Jose Maria Olazabal 2 up in the singles. It wasn't his performance on the course, though, that European captain **Tony Jacklin** *remembers. It was his performance off the course:*

The two teams were lined up behind me, and I began to introduce all the players again to the public, thanking them for entertaining everyone so royally over those three days. So I went down the line starting with Jack Nicklaus, the captain, and kept going, but when I got to Payne, I went brain-dead. I just couldn't remember his name. I remembered twenty-three names that day, but not his. Behind me, Nick Faldo said "Payne Stewart," but I was deaf as a post. Finally, somebody said it loud enough so that even I could hear it. Then, later that night, when I got to my hotel room, there was a picture under the door, saying, "Best wishes, Payne Stewart." It showed me what a good sense of humor he had.

Just a month after his triumph at Kemper Lakes, Payne was back to represent his country in the 1989 Ryder Cup matches at the Belfry Golf Club in Sutton Coldfield, England. No longer a rookie, Payne assumed more of a leadership role this time. Teammate **Mark McCumber** *offers proof:*

It was still dark out one day when we were awakened in the morning, basically shaken out of bed, by Bruce Springsteen's "Born in the U.S.A." echoing down the halls. Who else would it be but Payne? He had put it on like a miniature CD player in the hallway. Of players I think about who had a passion for the Ryder Cup since my career began, I would put him at the top of the list. He always talked about it. I remember numerous times when I played with him in one of the last groups on Sunday, where one of us would falter and not win the tournament, he would say, "Well, it's Ryder Cup points." He would regularly make reference to the top ten for Ryder Cup points. Conversely, when he rallied on Sunday to squeeze into the top ten, he would be excited because that would give him some points. Some guys just talk about it when there's about eight weeks or less to go. He talked about it come January. Other guys had goals of winning a major or a money title. His goal was to make the team. He was most comfortable when he was with a group of teammates.

Springsteen wasn't enough in 1989. The Europeans retained the
Cup with a 14–14 tie. This time, Payne earned only one point in
four matches, including a crucial singles loss to Olazabal. Yet as passionate as he was about Uncle Sam, he didn't let another disappointment ruin his post-match spirit. Ireland's **Christy O'Connor Jr.**,
who beat Fred Couples that day, explains:

After it was over and we had won, about two-thirds of the
members of both teams—maybe twenty of us—got
together, which was lovely, and had a wonderful time. We
played the harmonica and the spoons. It was a great party,
and it should happen a lot more at the Ryder Cup. Even
though Payne was a member of the losing team, his golf was
done, and he wanted to party. So we partied. He had tried
100 percent, which is what he always did in everything.

Two years later, the Americans were not in a partying mood. They
had work to do. They were now the ones anxious to end a drought.
Led by captain **Dave Stockton**, a two-time PGA Championship
winner, their opportunity would come on the Ocean Course at
Kiawah Island, South Carolina, in a confrontation forever known as
the War on The Shore. As Stockton points out, Payne was a big help:

From the point of view of being a cheerleader, he was one
of the solid ones. He was one player I didn't have to worry
about because I knew that he was going to get pumped up
just enough. He knew what was going on. He was a great
influence. What I really liked about him was that he
could be serious one moment and then pull off these

pranks the next. Take a Ben Hogan, who was serious all the time, or a Tommy Bolt who seemed like he was upset all the time. But here's a guy who could go both ways. During a practice round in South Carolina, we were out on the thirteenth hole when he untied my golf bag. So that when I took off on the cart, my beloved Ryder Cup golf bag crashes onto the cart path. I was ready to kill him. Next hole, he put ice water all over the seat. Lucky for me, I guess, my wife, Cathy, sat down in the cart before I did. He was mortified that Cathy was the one who took the brunt of the thing. He was just trying to keep me loose.

---

*With so much on the line, it wasn't easy to stay loose that year. Payne managed pretty well the first two days, collecting two and a half out of a possible three points. On Sunday, he wasn't so fortunate, although, as his opponent, **David Feherty**, remembers, Payne showed a lot of class:*

That was maybe the best golf I ever played in my life. I actually had it to two or three under par, which was completely unheard-of that week. When I got to four up with four to play and was walking to the fifteenth tee, the crowd was just enormous. They were jostling and bumping, yelling and shouting. People were patting me on the back, and whacking me. That Ryder Cup was unbelievable, the high temple of stress. I think that's where the tide turned on the intensity of the Ryder Cup. So, anyway, as I was walking through the crowd on the way to the seventeenth tee—I had lost two holes in a row—this fat lady marshal jumped in front of me and said, "Where do you think you're going?" I was kind of taken back and my caddie was already on the tee. Payne, who was walking down the fairway behind me, immediately broke stride and said, "Ma'am, I'd love you to stop him but he's playing me, okay?" He then put his arm around me and walked up to the tee with me.

He handled losing extremely well. People tend to remember Payne for the way he responded to winning the PGA in 1989. I really thought that was overplayed. Payne was one of the best losers I ever met. He really was. He was so gracious. For me, coming over here as an unknown player and his being the United States Open champion, he was great. Some of the things he said, people probably felt, well, he shouldn't have said them. But it was the sort of thing that if he said it *about* you, he had already said it *to* you.

Losing to Feherty in the first singles match of the day, which put his team behind, 9–8, did not stop Payne from being an enthusiastic cheerleader in a spirited U.S. performance that regained the Cup for the first time since 1983. Teammate **Chip Beck** *was very grateful for Payne's support:*

I was playing Ian Woosnam [who had won the Masters earlier that year], the number-one player in the world at the time. It was a critical match. As I went to the seventeenth tee, Payne was really encouraging me and excited about how I was playing. "You can beat this guy," he told me. "You can beat this guy. You've got him." I just remembered that and really appreciated it. [Beck defeated Woosnam 3&1, earning a key point in the Americans' 14½–13½ victory].

—◁◻◻▷—

In 1993, Payne was a member of the squad that went back to the Belfry. **Jim Gallagher Jr.** *was also on the team that retained the Cup, 15–13. Gallagher, a Ryder Cup rookie, credits Payne with playing a prominent role:*

I remember how inspirational he was. He was having fun, and he made the Ryder Cup fun for everyone else, he and [Paul Azinger]. I don't know if he said, "Jim, come on," or anything like that, but you could just feel the emotions he had. So you were emotional with him. The giant champagne bottle that they gave us after we had won ended up in my hands. I turned around and gave it to him, and he opened it on the eighteenth green. I wasn't sure I could get it opened, but he had no problem. We had a lot of great leaders, with [captain] Tom Watson and Lanny Wadkins and Raymond Floyd, but there's no doubt that Payne was a big part of that week. You always felt like you could go to Payne and talk to him, and he could tell you what to expect. You felt a little more at ease with him because he was closer to your age. He would have been a great captain.

—◁◻◻▷—

After failing to qualify for the team in 1995, Payne aimed to make it back in 1997. But his game didn't cooperate. Entering the PGA Championship at Winged Foot, he still had one last chance to impress Tom Kite enough to perhaps make him a captain's pick. The audition was not a successful one. Payne finished in a tie for twenty-ninth; Kite selected Lee Janzen and Fred Couples. Golf writer **Melanie Hauser**, *who had known Payne since his college days, covered the tournament:*

I was standing alone with him in the locker room when it had become clear that he was not going to be a pick. He was so disappointed. With all the experience he had and the ability to keep people loose and laughing, he felt that he could bring something special to Tom Kite's team. He was probably right. Face it, he bled red, white, and blue. How many times did you see him wearing red, white, and blue? But it was not to be.

Payne didn't dwell on disappointment. He instead turned his attention to making the 1999 team. He was so motivated, in fact, that almost any casual conversation could, at any moment, turn into a discussion of the Ryder Cup. ABC's **Mike Tirico** *bumped into him on Bourbon Street in New Orleans during the week of the 1999 COMPAQ Classic:*

We [some members of the ABC crew] walked into one of the first places and there's a guy in jeans and a T-shirt. Nobody's standing around him because nobody knows it's Payne. We just sat and had a soda and chatted for about a half hour. I vividly remember him talking about how important it was for him to make the Ryder Cup team, how he felt that with all the new guys that were going to be there, they needed a guy like him to really have the passion for what the event was all about. When I saw him at the U.S. Open two months later, after he had won, I said, "I remember talking to you about [the Ryder Cup] in New Orleans," and he said, "Yeah, I remember. I don't have to worry about making it [now]." I will never forget the intensity he had about making the team. He had a real appreciation for the team aspect of sports.

———⚙️———

*Once he made the team, he was determined to make his mark. Payne, who had tied for tenth when the U.S. Open was held at The Country Club in 1988, wasted little time in setting up a date to get reacquainted with the famed layout. Head professional **Brendan Walsh** made the arrangements:*

Payne came to play a practice round on July 5, right after he won the Open, with the *Boston Globe*'s Will McDonough, his agent Robert Fraley, and Chuck Cook. He had called and said he wanted to come up, so we put him out there in one of our member-guest tournaments. Any tour players who were potential Ryder Cuppers that called, we were going to get them on the course. Payne was very accommodating. He said, "I don't want to do anything to hurt the members."

He let people watch him, and he was nice to the kids. He decided to ride that day, so one of our assistants walked around and caddied for him. Afterward, Payne sat down on our little patio, where they later did all the celebrating, and talked to the members. Then when he came back on August 31 with other team members, he remembered the names of our staff and that impressed the heck out of me. Here's a guy who goes all over the world and he knew right away who we were. He was the only player to come twice before the competition. He was also one of a couple guys who wrote a thank-you note to the club after the matches were over.

———⚙️———

In the days leading up to the matches in late September, Payne had more on his mind than his own game. He was thinking about the rest of the team, and was eager to share his ideas with captain **Ben Crenshaw**:

A few weeks before the matches, my wife, Julie, and I were together, and Payne said, "I know one thing that's going to help us win this Ryder Cup, and that's a Ping-Pong table." We just looked at him a little bit and he said, "It's fun and it's a way we can be together. We can let off a little steam and it will help us take the edge off." So we got that table.

———

Ping-Pong table or not, for Payne, like the rest of the favored American squad, the battle of Brookline couldn't have started any worse. In Saturday morning's four-ball matches, Payne and his partner, Justin Leonard, lost to Lee Westwood and Darren Clarke. Payne took the defeat pretty hard, as Crenshaw's assistant, **Bruce Lietzke**, *can attest:*

After they lost their match on sixteen, I was sitting in my cart by the green, ready to give either Justin or Payne a ride back to the clubhouse. Payne did a couple of TV interviews real quick and started walking off by himself. So I pulled the cart beside him and offered him a ride. Boy, he just stared a hole right in the back of my head. He stopped and walked toward me at a pretty fast pace. I thought, "Oh, man, I might have said something that really made him mad." He put one foot up into the cart and then he got his face about a foot from mine. He had tears in his eyes. His only comment was, "I don't deserve to play this afternoon." That was probably one of the low moments in his great career, but it also just said a lot about someone who accepted his failures as well as all his wins. He had built his whole game around making the Ryder Cup these last two years, and yet he was willing to admit right there that he didn't feel like he was capable of helping the team. He didn't care about his own ego and his own record. I also remember the tears he had in his eyes as he spoke to the team Saturday night. I don't remember the particular words he said, but I do remember how emotional he was. He mentioned something about his sacrifices for the last two years and how he had not given up on the team.

—◁ᴜᴜ◊ᴜᴜ▷—

Shortly after his Saturday four-ball loss, Payne had calmed down enough to show that golf wasn't the only thing that mattered during Ryder Cup week. Former caddie **Mitch Kemper** *sets the scene:*

He was on the putting green with a lot of people watching. I was just standing there on the sidelines. Some kid came up to me, about fifteen years old, and he said, "You know Payne Stewart, don't you?" He had seen me say hello to him the day before. He then tells me that he has ADD, Attention Deficit Disorder, the same thing Payne has. He wanted to know if Payne would talk to him about it. Twenty minutes later, as Payne was getting ready to leave the green, I told him about the kid. It was no problem. "Hello, young man," he said to the kid. For at least five minutes, he totally gave this kid everything he had.

—◁ᴜᴜ◊ᴜᴜ▷—

The next day, the U.S. gave everything it had, staging a remarkable rally to capture the Cup for the first time since 1993. Down by four points entering Sunday's singles competition, the Americans won six matches in a row to take command. When Justin Leonard secured a halve with Jose Maria Olazabal by making a long putt at seventeen, it rendered Payne's match with **Colin Montgomerie** *meaningless. Still, by conceding Montgomerie's putt on the final hole, Payne won even more admirers, including his opponent:*

I have to say he couldn't have been more helpful to me in what were enormously stressful conditions for both of us. As early as the fourth tee, some of the spectators began heckling me relentlessly. That's when Stewart stepped in. He told me to let him know if there was anything he could say or do and that he would see to it that anyone causing trouble would be ejected. One hole later, it happened. As I approached my ball on the fifth fairway, a guy had to be thrown out. Payne was instrumental in having the man taken away. For all that, Payne wasn't trying any less hard to beat me. He was a real competitor. He had guts and courage, which is what the Ryder Cup is really all about—who better can handle the pressure. And Payne could handle it very well.

[After the match was over] Payne managed to locate my wife. She was the first person he went to see. He gave her a hug—Eimear told me this later—and said, "I just want you to know that what went on here should never have happened. I apologize for the fans' behavior." Now, my wife didn't really know Payne that well. She had walked with Tracey during our match, but for Payne to do what he did, to be so thoughtful in the midst of all that was going on, was amazing. When I heard this story from my wife, Payne leaped in our estimation. Eimear and I shall always be grateful for his support.[11]

———

NBC's **Mark Rolfing** *immediately went to work, talking to players about a comeback few people thought was possible. But when he reached Payne, Rolfing quickly discovered he wasn't going to get a formal interview. He didn't mind. Instead, he got something much more memorable:*

The last time I ever saw him was on the eighteenth green in the middle of that gigantic celebration. We had about forty to forty-five minutes left of airtime. So we were going to do interviews. I saw him out of the corner of my eye and went over to him and he knew what I was coming for. He looked over at me and took his bottle of champagne and poured it right on my head. That was kind of the interview. He gave me a big hug and we danced around a little bit.

———

Golf writer **Melanie Hauser** *was doing her job at Brookline when she and Payne made eye contact. That was all she needed:*

I was up on that little lawn area by the team room, talking to Justin Leonard, Ben Crenshaw, and a few other people. I then looked over and there was Payne on the porch. We looked at each other, and I gave him the thumbs-up. He gave me one back with that little wink and threw his head back like, "Don't you know it!" It was so totally him. He didn't have to say a word.

REFLECTIONS

He always reminded me of the rock band KISS. Those guys went on stage with their faces painted and put on a three-hour concert. Afterward, they went backstage, took a shower, put on their regular clothes, and walked in the streets unnoticed. When Payne went into the locker room or the hotel and put on long pants, a polo shirt, and a sweater, a lot of people didn't recognize him. He had the best of both worlds.

**—LEE TREVINO,
SENIOR PGA TOUR GOLFER**

Love him or loathe him, from his caddie to his coach, from his competitors to his critics, it's hard to find someone in the game of golf over the last two decades without something to say about Payne Stewart. For some, they cite a fleeting moment; for others, they reflect on a relationship that changed their lives forever. Following, in alphabetical order, are some thoughts from those who came away with a lasting impression of a player and personality who brought to his sport much more than he ever took away:

Peter Alliss, *veteran ABC and BBC broadcaster:*

In this day and age, when everyone was very automated, he was more of a free spirit. His golf swing was old-fashioned. It had width and balance and tempo, more like a swing from the 1930s and 1940s than the 1990s. He was a touch of ancient and modern, which I found very refreshing—an ancient swing but he behaved in a modern way with punching the air and high-fives, and had a brashness and youthfulness about him which was interesting considering he was forty-two years of age. He sometimes gave the impression that he was twenty years younger than that. He was outspoken, sometimes saying things that didn't make a whole lot of sense, but he had opinions and wasn't afraid to state them and stand by them or say, "That was a silly thing to say." One minute, he was in jeans and a cowboy shirt and the next, he seemed to be in a tuxedo. He was a bold player. He had to go for things. He never gave the impression of playing the game conservatively. That was all part of his charm. You never quite knew what was going to happen but you knew he was going to go gung-ho at everything.

———

Dave Anderson, *Pulitzer Prize–winning New York Times columnist:*

I was sitting on the fairway in front of the eighteenth green during the 1991 Ryder Cup at Kiawah some time after Mark Calcavecchia had blown a four-hole lead with four holes to go [to Colin Montgomerie] and wound up only getting a halve. Well, when Bernhard Langer missed the putt on eighteen clinching the Ryder Cup for the United States, all the players started celebrating. The first thing Payne did was go right over to Calcavecchia, who had been so distraught. Remember when he took a walk by the ocean; he thought he had blown the whole thing. And Payne said, "Your halve won it for us," which I thought was a great thing to say. Calcavecchia just nodded his head.

Billy Andrade, PGA *Tour player:*

I think it was my second year on the tour at Colonial. He was probably first on the money list and I was probably 250th. And I was kind of looking at the money list, checking it out, and, all of a sudden, I feel somebody on my shoulder. I look back and it's Payne. He says, "Well, where are you on the money list?" "Well, I'm way down," and he says, "Well, this is where you need to be." I said, "Yeah, I know, no kidding." He says, "Just play better," and he walked away, and I'll never forget that as long as I live.[12]

Larry Atwood, *Payne's high school basketball coach:*

I don't think it gets much better than receiving a golf glove from him. He was playing in the Skins Game in 1994, and my daughter, Leslie, who went to school with him, was in the crowd. He won the event, so as he was going off the green, he signed his glove, tossed it to her, and said, "Give this to your dad." It's a tremendous honor for him to think of me in that way.

―――⊶⊷―――

Paul Azinger, *PGA Tour player:*

Payne wasn't the most mechanically inclined person I ever knew. I'll never forget the mistake he made when he told me the story of the time he started his bass boat in his garage. Payne showed me that bass boat; he was so proud of it. I knew he wasn't much of a fisherman at the time, and I didn't know how often he would use this boat. One day, he jumped in the boat, and I guess, feeling bad that he hadn't started the engine in a while, just put the key in the ignition and turned it over. He first took the time to squeeze the bulb—he knew that much—to prime the engine, and he turned the key over and the motor started and it was so loud. And he said he was so happy it kicked on, and he kept revving the engine. He said that for five minutes, the thing just ran like a champ. He kept it going. An outboard engine cannot run without water, and it exploded. Payne said he freaked out, flames hit the ceiling. He leaped out of the boat and grabbed the hitch and ran out of the garage to keep the house from burning down. And then he made the mistake of telling me. And I told everybody I knew about that. I cut an ad out of a fishing magazine for an outboard motor, and I taped it to his locker at the next tournament and I wrote a big note on top, "Just Add Water."

I first met Payne in 1982 on the putting green in Hattiesburg, Mississippi [at the Magnolia Classic]. It was before he donned his trademark knickers and Tam

O'Shanter hat. Yet he still stood out. What I had mistaken for earrings were actually acupuncture needles. They were in there to help improve his concentration. It must have worked because he won the event. In the post-victory interview, he announced to the world that the tour needed more blond-haired, blue-eyed guys, and I remember thinking, "Who in the heck is this guy?"[13]

⟶⟶⟶

Paul Azinger:

One of the funniest things he ever did to me, we were playing in the U.S. Open in 1989. I was just ahead of him in this buffet-style lunch that they had, and I got the last piece of chocolate cake. I laughed at him, and went and sat down at the booth; he was sitting with someone else. He walked by me, put his hand over the cake, and said, "Man, it's still warm, too." And I reached my hand over there, and he just smashed my hand down into the cake. He walked off, laughing. I said, "You dog, you got me."[14]

⟶⟶⟶

Andy Bean, PGA *Tour player:*

There was someone else's car in my parking place every day [at the Byron Nelson Classic one year]. I had one of the past champions' spots. Finally, one afternoon, I was actually walking back to the hotel because it was only fifty yards from the clubhouse, and I saw Payne go to the car that was in my spot. I said, "What the devil are you doing parking in my place? When you win this tournament, you'll have a place, too." I was just carrying on with him, and he said, "Well, I didn't think you'd mind." I told him, "You park there tomorrow, and I'm going to have your car towed," and he looked at me, "You wouldn't." It wasn't parked there the next day. In 1990, he won that tournament and had his own spot.

Guy Boros, *PGA Tour player:*

I didn't know him well until we went on a fishing trip north of Vancouver three years ago. I had always heard from other people that he wasn't the nicest fellow and a bit standoffish, but we just hit it off. Then we played the first two days together last year in Vancouver. I never had as much fun playing with anyone in two days. I laughed the whole way around. He knew what kind of struggle I had been going through, and he told me I was too good a player not to still be out [on the tour] competing. A lot of players wouldn't care, but he took the time to tell me that. I think I even hugged him after we had finished.

Don Brauer, *friend:*

I'll always remember the way he treated my daughter, Megann. When she was eight years old, we took her to see the Honda Classic. This was in 1989. We had never met Payne, but we started following him in the first round. She liked him because he wore knickers; she even nicknamed him that. On Friday, she wanted to give him something for good luck. Her idea was to use a coin from her grandfather's collection. She picked out a dime, and gave it to Payne, who used it as his ball marker for the rest of the tournament. He finished fourth at Bay Hill the following week and then won the MCI the next month. Payne later sent Megann a letter, thanking her for the lucky coin and telling her they had to remain friends forever. I was impressed. Here's a guy who is a star, yet he wasn't self-centered. He was considerate to the people who cared for him. And they remained friends until the day he died.

Mark Brooks, *PGA Tour player:*

In the media room after the Ryder Cup victory at Brookline, I thought he handled himself the best of all the players. I didn't feel that he was defensive about the incident at seventeen [where U.S. players stormed the green prematurely, before Jose Maria Olazabal had a chance to putt]. He showed a lot of wisdom and character in realizing [what had happened]. If it had happened five or seven years earlier, I think he would have taken a more defensive stand. He never excused it.

Reagan Brown, *SMU classmate:*

I was [at the 1995 Shell Houston Open] with my youngest son, who was about eight or nine years old, about the same age as Payne's daughter. He was getting ready to hit on one of the par-threes, and was starting to make a move on the field. I then said to him, "That's no hill for a stepper," and he starts to look around because that was something that our golf coach, Earl Stewart, always said to us, meaning that this was not a difficult shot for somebody who is a player. He came up to me and gave a golf ball to my son. It was in the middle of a tournament, and yet he still had time to chat with us. He then hit a great shot and went on to win the tournament the next day.

Brad Bryant, former PGA Tour player:

I kind of suffered from a bad back, and that's part of the reason I'm retired now. He was always on me about losing weight because he figured that would help my back. This went on for about four or five years and became kind of a running gag. Last year, I walked into the locker room at Disney, hunched over because my back had been hurting real bad that week. "Your back's hurting you again, isn't it?" he said. I said, "Yeah, it is." He said, "Well, if you'd get rid of that belly of yours, your back wouldn't hurt you so bad. I've been after you all these years." That was the last thing he ever said to me. We laughed about it, and then I wished him luck at the Tour Championship.

Jim Colbert, Senior PGA Tour player:

A few years ago, I was playing him in the Wendy's Three-Tour Challenge in Las Vegas, when it came down to the last hole, and our match was the swing match. If I beat him, the seniors were going to win the deal. But he beat me on the last hole; I might have bogeyed it. When it was over, I shook his hand. He put his arm around me and said: "That was for my dad." I had beaten his dad two years in a row in the mid-sixties in the semifinals of the state amateurs in Kansas and Missouri. Payne was only about eight or nine at the time, but he remembered. I played a lot of golf with Bill Stewart. His golf game was just the opposite of Payne's. Payne had a pure swing and he hit all these great-looking golf shots, while his dad didn't hit great golf shots but was a great putter and a great competitor.

His hands warmed by mittens, Payne discusses some Pebble Beach strategy with partially hidden TV star Don Johnson. (AP/Wide World Photos; Walt Zeboski)

Chuck Cook, *Payne's longtime swing coach:*

I always felt a little bit like Butch Harmon [Tiger Woods's instructor] when we were giving our lessons. I'd be going, "Good shot, good shot. That's better." Payne told me when we first started working that his dad had told him never to change his golf swing. And so I was picked to be the keeper of that magnificent action.

I never met a man who was more comfortable in his own skin. It didn't matter whether he was with royalty or people who were less fortunate. I remember in Monte Carlo, Princess Stephanie had met Payne at a formal soiree. He had a tuxedo that wasn't quite like everybody else's. She said, "That Payne Stewart is quite the cat's meow." Payne loved that story.

In 1992 Payne had to return the U.S. Open trophy that he had won in 1991 and had to go to Pebble Beach for a media day. He invited me to go with him. We were sitting in the Lodge at Pebble Beach, and this boisterous guy came up to us and said, "That guy said you're Payne Stewart. I don't believe it." Payne said, "If I go get the U.S. Open trophy, will you keep filling it up with whatever I want to drink? Will that prove it to you?" And the guy says, "You bet I will." So Payne brought the U.S. Open trophy over and turned to the bartender and said, "Bring us some bottles of Cristal champagne." We sat there and drank several bottles of Cristal champagne. Cristal champagne is very expensive, but at the Lodge at Pebble Beach, it is *really* expensive. This guy may be the only guy I know who wishes he hadn't met Payne Stewart, because he's a lot poorer now. We drank into the wee hours of the night out of that old cup and we walked out, and Payne said, "Let's go over by the eighteenth green at Pebble," and we walked over there and sat down on this retaining wall that was there, just covered with sand, and there was a twenty-five-foot drop, and sat the trophy down right in the middle of this sand. It could have fallen over and been gone forever. And we talked for hours. We talked about life.[15]

———

John Cook, *PGA Tour player:*

We were invited by Ken Griffey Jr. [to a Seattle Mariners game in Tampa, Florida]. So Payne and I, Mark O'Meara [and a few others] went. Junior's up a couple of times and strikes out. This might be the worst game of his life. Every time he walks back to the dugout, Payne is up and giving him the business. About the fourth or fifth inning, we take a walk out to center field because there weren't that many people there. Junior gets a walk, and they try to hit and run but [he gets thrown out in a rundown]. Now, you can just tell that Junior doesn't want to come out to center field because we're out there. He walks out and Payne starts running back and forth, across the row. "Junior, does this look familiar?"[16]

———

Nathaniel Crosby, *1981 U.S. Amateur champion:*

In 1986, Davis Love's rookie year, I got an exemption into the San Diego Open at Torrey Pines. Payne and I were playing a practice round on the front nine of the South course with Davis, and nobody had heard of Davis. He didn't win the NCAAs or anything. Payne just couldn't believe this guy. He's hitting it fifty yards by both of us and straight on every hole, which he couldn't fathom. I think on a couple of holes, in fact, Davis hit a one-iron past our drives. Payne was probably hitting it about 265 and Davis was hitting it well over 300. Payne was starting to get upset about it. He'd say to me, "Well, let's see how close he gets it to the pin. See, he doesn't hit it very close." So he quit after nine. He couldn't handle it. He told Davis, "Oh, I forgot I got to do something," and went off.

⚊⚊⚊

Jayne Custred, *sportswriter for the* Houston Chronicle:

At the 1996 Players Championship, I was there to do a big blowout piece on Payne for the Shell Open program. He had won the tournament the year before. On Saturday, after his round, in which he hadn't played particularly well, he came off the course and wasn't in a great mood. In fact, he walked off to the other side of the scoring tent, away from the reporters, which really wasn't like him. He started stalking off down the road where the locker room was. I ran after him. When I caught up, I said, "Payne, I need a few minutes. Anytime today, tomorrow, whenever you want to do it. It's for the cover piece of the Shell Houston Open." He kept walking, didn't slow down at all, finally saying, "I'm doing a conference call with them Monday morning." I said, "I understand that, but they want some more in-depth stuff and I'll be on an airplane at that time." He said, "Well, I guess you have a problem, don't you?" Then he kept walking to the locker room.

I was so incensed. And the thing was, he and I had a pretty good relationship. I went back to the media center and started bad-mouthing him to every person I saw. I got on the phone and called Burt Darden at the Shell Houston Open, speaking very loudly, "I don't know who he thinks he is, but that is it. I will not beg him for an interview." Then I suddenly looked up and Payne was standing at the entrance to the media center. I hung up the phone. He walked over and said, "I'm here to apologize. That was uncalled for. You were just trying to do your job. I'm in a bad mood and took it out on you. I'll sit here and give you as much time as you need." We sat there and had a really good interview, and from then on, we had a great relationship.

———

Burt Darden, *director of communications for the Houston Golf Association:*

In 1995, after he won here, he went back to the public hospitality tent we called the Bunker, signed autographs, and got on the stage to sing the Village People song, "YMCA." It was a hoot. He, in fact, went out to the Bunker and played almost every night. He must have signed two hundred autographs that day.

———

Jay Delsing, *PGA Tour player:*

When I was first on the tour, I was coming down the stretch on Friday trying to make the cut. It turned out I was way off on the number and because of that, I played too aggressively, missing a cut I shouldn't have missed. Payne told me, "Don't ever worry about the cut. Play the hole you're on and do the best you can."

—⁂—

Brian DePasquale, *USGA media staff member:*

My first Open was at Baltusrol in 1993, and he had one of those press conferences early in the week. So I was sent to look for him by the driving range, and then ran right into him. We didn't know each other from Adam, and right away he went into this spoof on how he had gotten hit in the front teeth with a seven-iron on the range. His teeth were all bloody, and he was holding his mouth. He played it perfectly. He must have had it all planned. He certainly had me believing the whole thing. I offered to take him to medical but he said he was okay.

We went into the media tent and when people saw him holding the towel, they all bought it, too, thinking they had a story that could break the usual monotony before a tournament gets under way. He went through the whole thing of what happened. Then he pulled the fake teeth right out of his mouth. Everyone gasped, and he started laughing. He was all happy with himself that he had pulled it off. From that point forward, every Open he and I would remind each other of that incident. He was different from the other guys, especially for such a high-pressure week. He'd usually kid around with you.

—⁂—

Without the Tam O'Shanter hat and the trademark plus-fours, Payne Stewart blended in with the crowd, even when he was on the golf course, as he is here, playing a practice round at Shoal Creek in Birmingham, Alabama, before the 1990 PGA Championship. (AP/Wide World Photos; Dave Martin)

Bruce Devlin, ESPN *golf analyst:*

My wife and I went to Morocco ten or twelve years ago to play in King Hassan's tournament [the Hassan II Trophy]. Payne came without Tracey, bringing his mom instead. He treated her like royalty, dancing with her, going to every cocktail party with her, being totally attentive. In ten days, I don't think that ten seconds went by without him knowing where she was. He impressed my wife and me more by being the son of a lady than by the way he played golf.

—————

Jaime Diaz, Sports Illustrated *senior writer:*

Payne was exasperating to a lot of his friends. He did silly and annoying things. But they all liked him because later he would apologize. He was self-effacing; that was his saving grace. I was talking to Paul Azinger in the pressroom one night in San Diego. I asked him, "Why is Payne Stewart your best friend? To me, you guys are so different. You're considerate and you think deep thoughts, and Payne is sort of shallow and selfish." He kind of laughed and said, "You know, many guys don't like Payne. Sometimes, I just catch myself going, 'Why am I this guy's friend?' But there's just something about him, something that's totally harmless. He's just like a kid you want to put your arm around and kind of guide. I laugh when I'm around him." To me, that summed it all up.

In the mid-1990s, it must have crossed his mind that he was done. He looked like he was done. He wasn't practicing much. He was getting heavy. He looked like a satisfied, rich golfer who had everything he wanted. Even the excess of that huge house of his seemed to reflect a guy who didn't have it together in other ways. But, in the last few years of his life, he showed remarkable discipline. It's hard to change your personality at thirty-eight or thirty-nine years old, but I think he did just that, and it was very admirable. Regardless of his ability or the way he dressed, to me, that's his lasting legacy.

Brad Faxon, PGA *Tour player:*

He didn't like to hit a thousand balls. He would rather be on the course with the money game. It didn't matter who you were playing with, two other tour players or two guys out of the cart barn, he was going to have some fun. I learned a lot from that. He'd have a Coke or he'd be chewing his tobacco. It was like he loved his job, but he wasn't afraid to make it fun, whereas some guys say, "I'm not going to smile today because I'm a tour player." I remember [at the 1984 Walt Disney World Golf Classic] we were in one of the last groups together on Sunday. I was very nervous, never having been in contention. I ended up finishing third. Payne was very nice to me. I was absolutely the slowest player on the planet, and we got warned for being out of position. But Payne never said a thing to me. He had been there. He said, "Good playing, hey, it's a great way to finish your year." He was very complimentary toward me, and we might have even had a beer afterward.

Bruce Fleisher, Senior PGA Tour player:

I ran with Payne a lot in the early 1980s. He was incredible with my daughter, Jessica. She knew him as "the Tickle Monster." He would tickle her and make funny faces. She just flipped over him. It started when she was about three or four years old and it continued for a long time.

Eric Fredricksen, executive director of the Houston Golf Association:

We were on the way to the airport after he had won the 1995 Houston Open in the play-off with Scott Hoch, who had blown a pretty big lead. He called his mom first from the car. He shared the victory with her and got pretty emotional. Then he called Tracey and told her how much he had felt for Scott, that he hoped that it wouldn't hurt the friendship they had developed, and how much it meant to him that Sally [Scott's wife] had been the first person to call to congratulate Tracey. He was crying.

Shawn Freeman, head professional at the Bill and Payne Stewart Municipal Golf Course in Springfield, Missouri:

In preparing for Payne's arrival at the course last July, we wanted to rope off certain areas so he had easy access to the pro shop and the driving range. I made this elaborate thing to get ready for him. He was supposed to let someone know when he was there so we could pick him up with a cart and take him to the driving range. In classic Payne style, he showed up a little early, grabbed the U.S. Open trophy he had brought with him, and carried it up to the pro shop. People swarmed all over him, so I was concerned with how he felt about that. I tried to back people off and give him some space, but he wouldn't have any of that. You could tell he was glad to be around his hometown people. He didn't feel more important than the people around him. He was scheduled to be there for an hour and a half, and he stayed probably double that, until everyone left. He signed every autograph.

Chuck Gerber, *coordinator of the Skins Game:*

Right before he won the 1991 U.S. Open at Hazeltine, he came up to me one day and asked, as only Payne could in those days, how somebody gets into the Skins Game. He said, "I guess you have to be either a client of IMG [a sports agency] or Don Ohlmeyer's best friend." [Ohlmeyer was the event's founder.] And I said, "No, Payne, you have to do something that is worthy in the game of golf, like win a major." And we left. Then he won at Hazeltine and I sent him a note, saying, "I guess that's worthy. Would you like to play in the Skins Game?" He called and said, "Absolutely. I'm in." He became the first three-time winner, doing it three years [1991–1993] in a row. What I remember most from his appearances was his relationship with Paul Azinger. Paul was really hurt—this was right before the cancer was diagnosed—and I saw a side of Payne Stewart I had not seen. You could see the compassion he felt for his friend. You could see it in his eyes.

David Graham, *Senior PGA Tour player:*

He and I used to joke quite a lot about how he kind of wanted to follow me around because I won the U.S. Open in 1981 and he won it in '91, and I won the PGA in 1979 and he won it in '89. He always said we were exactly ten years apart, not only in age, but also in winning our majors. He kept joking to me about how he wanted me to win another major so that, ten years down the road, he'd win the same one, too.

Melanie Hauser, *columnist for golfweb.com:*

I first met him when he was a junior in college. I had called him on the telephone in his hotel room because I had missed him on the course. The next day, he won the tournament. I don't remember which one. Anyway, we were on the back porch of the clubhouse. I walked up and introduced myself and he was very cocky. I kind of laughed to myself, thinking, "Okay, let's just deal with this kid." And, for twenty years, I did. We picked at each other constantly. There were times when you just really wanted to smack him because he would be such a smart-aleck but, at the same time, he would temper it with one of those winks and grins, and you really had to laugh even though you knew what he had done was pushing the line. He did get more mellow in the last few years, but even last year, he called into *Viewer's Forum* on the Golf Channel, letting a reporter have it on live TV. He didn't like something that reporter had written. I remember walking past Payne a short time after that, and I said, "Please, if you're ever mad at me, don't get me on national TV." He looks at me and says, "Don't ever tick me off." He had a wink, of course. But I knew he was serious, too. He held you accountable as much as you held him accountable.

Orel Hershiser, *baseball pitcher:*

Talk about a guy who just sucked everything out of life and got everything there was for it, and then really got squared away with God near the end of his life. It was so exciting to see that.[17]

Joe Inman, *Senior PGA Tour player:*

When I saw him, he always remembered my name when I was not really anyone that he should be expected to remember. After all, I wasn't even playing golf on the tour anymore. I was a rep for Ping. I was promoting equipment. I saw certain younger players out there on the tour who were starting when I was finishing who didn't even make an effort. That didn't bother me at all.

It's just that when somebody does, that was the kind of thing that sticks out.

—⟨⟨⟨⟩⟩⟩—

Terry Jastrow, president of Jack Nicklaus Productions:

I saw Ben Crenshaw on the practice tee one day at Pebble Beach just mesmerized by a player, just frozen, watching every move. I kind of knew it was Payne Stewart, but I didn't know too much about him. I walked up to Ben and said, "What are you doing?" and he said, "I can't stop watching this guy swing. He's got the most perfect left-arm movement. I think the movement of his left arm is a piece of art, golf art. I can't stop watching how pure and lovely and flawless it is." It was a beautiful movement.

I love Payne Stewart and, by the way, I say that in the present tense. Because he lives on. His personality and what he meant to the game very much live on. He's up there playing with David Marr and Old Tom Morris. He's got Jimmy Demaret two down at the turn. I love him because he kept it a game. It was his life, his business. But there was a playfulness about Payne. He tried as hard as he could but he never took himself or it all too seriously. He was always polite and never condescending.

I thought Payne would work as well in the streets of Paris as he would in the streets of Paris, Texas. He'd have a drink or two with you and have a little something in his mouth he was chewing on. In our day of superstars and pro-grammed athletes, I thought he was always a little bit like a Tony Lema, in that there was charm and a devilishness about him. I always loved his style, and his idiosyncrasies. He was fun, and you can't say that about a lot of the guys.

Whatever producers and directors say, they have people that they like and people they don't like. I thought he was good television. He was unique and eventful and I would go out of my way to tell the Payne Stewart story whenever I could, and often, it was easy to do.

The week before the 1998 U.S. Open at the Olympic Club, Payne played one of our *Shell's Wonderful World of Golf* matches against Nick Price in Aruba. He actually prepared for San Francisco all week at a Caribbean island. He even did a clinic that week for junior golfers there. We've done twenty-eight matches in the series, and not once had we had a player offer to do a clinic for junior golfers at the location. The thing went on, as I recall, for a couple of hours. He would hang out, hit shots, and talk to these kids. On the day before the match, he invited me to play in his practice round. "Go get your clubs, I'll see you on the first tee at ten o'clock," he said. I'm not a very good chipper, so at the twelfth hole, he said, "Now put that ball down here and let me show you how to do it." I remember he was talking about the importance of timing. "One, two, three," he said. To this day, I think about that chip-shot routine—one, two, three.

—————

Peter Jacobsen, PGA *Tour player:*

He brought to the game a level of excitement I think that is missing in the game today. And, hopefully, the young players will realize that was Payne's legacy and try to emulate not only his swing and not only his demeanor on the golf course, but that charismatic attitude that he brought to his playing partners and to the golf fans. He was interesting to be around. . . . He became more of a mentor in his later years to the younger players, people like Tiger Woods and Lee Janzen and David Duval. And that's what I think Payne always wanted to be because his father was a mentor to a lot of people, including Payne. I'm proud of what he leaves behind.

I remember, in 1984, when Payne and I were in a play-off at the Colonial, my father was on his death bed, I thought. And I ended up beating Payne. He was so warm and so comforting to me, saying how happy he was that I won the tournament and that "I hope your father's watching. I hope your father's well. I hope he lives many, many years," which he did. He lived another nine years. And his father, ironically, passed away shortly after that [tournament in 1985]. So because of that, I will always be intertwined with Payne. Because of our relationships with our fathers. The kindness and the warmth he showed me, I'll never forget.[18]

Drue Johnson, *director of golf at Hickory Hills Country Club in Springfield, Missouri:*

He was awfully good to me. I asked him to play a practice round with me at Riviera Country Club in Los Angeles when I qualified for the 1995 PGA Championship. He said it was no problem, almost like he expected it. During the round, I was very impressed that he would stop and talk to people he didn't know on his way from the green to the next tee. I remember him speaking to an elderly lady in a wheelchair who was just by herself along the ropes.

Mitch Kemper, *Payne's caddie in 1982 and 1983:*

The only time I ever saw Payne intimidated was during the 1983 Los Angeles Open, which they held at Rancho Park because they were getting Riviera ready for the PGA Championship later in the year. Payne played pretty well the first two days, and got paired on Saturday with Arnold Palmer. I remember he hit it over the green at ten, and there were these people all over the place. We literally couldn't chip up. Payne was shaking in his boots. He finished with a 73 that day. He was intimidated by the crowd and by the legend itself. Another time, in the Crosby tournament at Pebble Beach, he was two under going into the eighteenth hole, the long par-five. He hit a good drive and had about 250 to the flag. He asked me what I thought, and I said, "You could get a three-wood there." He said: "What would Palmer do, Bud?" I said, "Palmer would go for it." He whipped out that three-wood. He got home in two.

Peter Kessler, *host of* Golf Talk Live *on* The Golf Channel:

The first couple of times we met in the studio, you got the feeling that he had lots of things going on, yet they weren't fully under control. That fleeting impression that I had, however, went away fast, and that was the thing with Payne. He was a really handsome guy and he looked great in clothes and had a really great smile and a quick sense of humor. So you could get a really surfacy kind of read on him if you didn't pay enough attention. I'm not so sure he changed as much as I just grew to appreciate the guy. On one of our *Academy Live* shows, during one segment with an instructor we had on, he agreed to make a complete fool out of himself as though he had never hit a golf ball before. This was to demonstrate something about the swing for our viewers. The point is that he was willing to be silly. Not every player would allow that. Yet a moment later, also on cue, he swung just like Sam Snead.

———

Peter Kostis, *CBS commentator and golf instructor:*

My first recollection of him was at the St. Andrews Country Club in Boca Raton, Florida. Payne, who was playing in the Far East at the time, had come to see Bob Toski for a lesson. He was kind of out there with some of the stuff he was doing to help him become a better player, like an earring in one ear that he had gotten through acupuncture. He thought that it would improve his concentration. He was so serious about improving his golf game to the extent that he would use any means possible. It was kind of funny that when Payne left, Bob said that if this kid knew how good he really was, he wouldn't need all that other stuff, like the earring and all this existential thinking that was going on in his head. He was that good.

———

Bill Kratzert, *ESPN golf commentator:*

You know when something's going wrong with a guy. It wasn't like I was telling everybody, but Payne kind of knew. "You're not yourself," he said to me one day in the late 1980s. "Anything you want to talk about?" I said, "Well, it's nothing that doesn't happen to a lot of people." I was going through a divorce. So I went into the details, and he said, "Not everyone is as fortunate as I have been," referring to Tracey. He said, "If there's anything I can do or if you need to call somebody just to talk, whether it's at a tournament or when I'm at home, don't feel like you're putting me out." For a guy to offer that and not be so consumed by his own game, I was very appreciative. He offered that to me when he really didn't have to.

Bruce Lietzke, *PGA Tour player:*

Virtually every time I got paired with Payne, he would bring up the fact that I had beaten his dad in an amateur tournament, the Trans-Mississippi tournament, in Dallas in 1972. I won that match fairly handily and never thought about it again until Payne came out on the tour. He would always have a little sarcastic remark about my beating his dad in only the way Payne could do it.

Mike Lupica, New York Daily News *sports columnist:*

It [the last two hours of the 1999 U.S. Open] became so emotional, and I had nothing against Phil Mickelson, but somehow there was such a purity to watching Payne go after this because I had been at Olympic and had seen him get hit by one of the great final rounds [Lee Janzen's 68]. He was so great in losing that Open, staying in the tent until the last question had been asked. You listened to him, and as much pain as he was feeling, he was like he had won because of the way he handled it. Now you have all that history coming into the final round at Pinehurst. I just got wrapped up in it, and was rooting as hard for him as if I would have been rooting for a friend. I brought my sons in and told them why it mattered and told them how he had missed the putt on eighteen the year before. I got as excited watching him as I got watching Jack Nicklaus at the 1986 Masters. Then I started trying to remember anyone who had ever missed the putt on the Open one year and then come back to win the next. It would be like Steve McNair having one more play in next year's Super Bowl, and this time, they score.

―⸬―

Bill Macatee, USA/CBS *golf host:*

Of all the upper-echelon players that I've come across, Payne had more of a regular-guy quality than almost anybody. Payne reminds me of the guys I used to go water skiing with or play nine holes of golf with when I was growing up in Texas. He was so accessible. One year, we were at a barbecue at a doctor's private home during the week of the Greensboro Open in North Carolina. He asked me how I was doing, and then said, "You don't know who I am, do you?" Of course, I did, but he was that down-to-earth. Here was a guy who had already won a U.S. Open, and he still thought that maybe somebody didn't know who he was. I wasn't really close to him, but you always felt like you could be. The fact that he's not around anymore, you feel cheated if you didn't take advantage of the window of opportunity.

<hr />

Carol Mann, LPGA *Hall of Famer:*

He was giving a clinic at Baltimore Country Club, where my dad was a member. I happened to be in town, so I went out over there. There was a thunderstorm; everybody had to go indoors. Yet, sitting on a stool at the bar and drenched with a towel around him, he conducted a beautiful Q&A with all these children. It was very sweet. At the time—this was the late 1980s—Payne had only revealed the side of him that some people did not find appealing. Yet on this day, he was being so attentive to these children. I knew then that there was more to Payne Stewart than he had shown the general public, the media, and maybe even his fellow players. He became endearing to me. I thought he was maybe kind of an insecure, defensive guy, but underneath, the real Payne Stewart was this person sitting on the stool.

<hr />

Payne enjoys a dad's dance with his daughter, Chelsea. (Photo courtesy of Susan Daniel)

Steve Melnyk, *ABC golf commentator:*

From the broadcast perspective, he was a delight as an interview. He was not a book-bright person, but he had a lot of common sense and street smarts, and he promoted himself extremely well. He was refreshing. He was honest. The camera was friendly to him. People had a sense of identity with him. On the practice tee, he would always tell me what he was doing, what he was working on regarding his game. He was very open in communicating to all of us on the television side things that could obviously complement the broadcast.

Phil Mickelson, PGA *Tour player:*

The thing that I remember most about Payne Stewart is at the end of [1998], he was not happy with the way he had been playing. So he did not sign on with any equipment company. He played whatever he wanted to play because he felt it was more important for him to play his best, for him to be fulfilled. He had made enough money. He went out and won AT&T and the U.S. Open. I thought that showed what he was all about. It wasn't about money to him. It was about performing well and winning.[19]

—⟨∿⟩—

Jim Morris, *close friend from Springfield:*

We were headed back from the 1993 Pro-Am in Pebble Beach, which we had just won. We obviously had celebrated a little bit, especially Payne. We were supposed to play with Donald Trump the next day. He wanted us to fly in with him but we had my van, and since Payne was playing down in the Bob Hope tournament the following week, we decided to drive. So he went to sleep in the back end; I used to keep a mattress back there. Coming through Pasadena, at about 1:30 or 2:00 in the morning, I was a little sleepy. So I pulled into a Jack in the Box, and there was nobody in it. I thought they were just getting ready to close.

My wife, Connie, and I went in to go to the bathroom and to get a cup of coffee. Payne was still in the van. But when I got out of the bathroom, there was a guy with a .38 pointed at Connie's forehead. Another guy had an Uzi. I obviously was scared and lost my temper. My wife finally screamed at me to do whatever they said, which I did. I gave them my billfold, which had a few hundred dollars. They took off. As soon as the door slammed, someone dialed 911 and the cops were there in no time at all. Suddenly, Payne climbs out of the van. He had seen the flashing lights. He says: "What's the party all about?" We kept on going to the desert and played golf the next day.

Payne had kind of taken me on as his mentor, sometimes referring to me as his second father. On the tour, he didn't get to spend too much time with his dad, which always bothered him. So he spent a lot of time asking me about Billy. I remember him saying, "I wish I had had the time with him man-to-man rather than just father to son." The biggest thing I remember about when we won the Pebble Beach tournament in 1993 was that his dad would have been there, not me, had he not passed away. Walking down the eighteenth fairway, we were both saying how it wasn't just the two of us playing. There were three of us playing, and that's why we won.

Byron Nelson, golfing legend:

When I went down to visit him, I would watch him practice. We'd have general conversations about the game, although I didn't teach him. I thought he had a wonderful swing, very fluid. The motion of the body and the arms together was excellent, and he never looked like he was hitting the ball very hard because his rhythm was so good. The arms and hands and the club were working right with the rhythm of his body. I think that was one of the great things about his game. His attitude was also very good. He had a great respect for the game, and he was very friendly and easy to be around.

―⌐◆⌐―

David Ogrin, PGA *Tour player:*

I was astounded when he so boldly displayed the "What Would Jesus Do" bracelet and credited God with his accomplishment—because he was Payne Stewart, almost the prototype of what every player aspires to be on the PGA Tour. He had won three major championships, lived in a big house, signed big endorsement contracts. Everybody knew who he was, especially in the uniform he wore out there. I never got to ask him about the WWJD bracelet, and I regret that.

―⌐◆⌐―

Jerry Pate, *former PGA Tour player:*

He became extremely interested in other people and his family, things that matter to humanity other than winning another U.S. Open trophy. You can take those U.S. Open trophies and line them up from Orlando to Los Angeles, and they're not as important as the fact that he got his personal life in order and knew what his priorities were—his faith first, his family second, and golf third.

―⌐◆⌐―

Gary Player, *Senior PGA Tour player:*

I wrote him a letter to congratulate him on winning last year's U.S. Open. He won an incredible Open. He just hung in there, and I was so proud of the way he did it. He came to me at the British Open a few weeks later at Carnoustie, looked me in the eye, put his arm around me, and shook my hand in a very warm way. "I really appreciated that letter and I'm keeping it in a very special place," he said. Invariably, I write letters when guys win major championships. Most guys are appreciative when I do that, but he had a special thanks in the way he said it. He made you feel good. And he loved international golf, which I think is so important.

Cathy Reynolds, *former LPGA Tour player who grew up in Springfield:*

I always laughed when he got on tour and became the knickers boy because he was a stripes-and-plaid boy growing up. I used to ask him if he got dressed in the dark all the time. He was like, "Why? Is there something wrong?" He didn't know. He never cared about how he dressed when we were kids.

He was like my brother. When we were seven or eight years old, we would constantly hit shots together at Hickory Hills that were to win the U.S. Open; that was always the big thing. We would putt, chip, hit hundreds of balls from fifty yards, then go back to seventy-five yards, and then a hundred. There were always little contests.

Jimmy Roberts, ESPN/ABC *reporter:*

When I first started to cover golf for ESPN in the early 1990s, I remember seeing Payne at Augusta. Needing him for a story, I walked up to him at the Oak Tree and said, "Hi, Payne, my name is Jimmy Roberts from ESPN. Do you have a minute?" He looked at me and said, "Yeah, but make it quick." My gut instinct was to say, "Never mind. I don't really need your time so badly that I need to be insulted." Because it was so demeaning, and that's the way he was. A year later, the very same thing happened again. I did the interview, but I do remember being angry.

Eventually, though, a relationship formed. When I needed to talk to him, he wasn't dismissive. I don't know if there's anybody I've ever covered with whom I've ever experienced more of a turnaround. During the week of the PGA at Valhalla in 1996, there was a benefit screening for *Tin Cup*, in which I had a small part. When my scene, where I basically played myself, came up on the screen, Payne gave me a good-natured ribbing. He obviously felt that we had established a good enough relationship that he could give me a hard time. But I never felt there was an attempt by Payne to co-opt me. I felt that he was just trying to get it right.

———

Chi Chi Rodriguez, Senior PGA Tour *player:*

He had the most flawless swing I ever saw in my life. I don't know how he didn't win everything. But I will always remember him, not as a great golfer, but as the guy who gave the $500,000 to his church and donated all his money [$108,000 from winning the 1987 Bay Hill Invitational to the Florida Hospital Circle of Friends, in memory of his father]. I won't remember him as a midget with his golf clubs. I'll remember him as a giant with his heart.

Mark Rolfing, *NBC on-course commentator:*

One thing I really liked about Payne, and this is not the case with a lot of players on the PGA Tour, was that he listened to the questions and answered them very well. I used to stop and get myself organized before talking to him, even if it was for just thirty seconds rather than winging it like I do with some of the guys. I knew he would listen to the questions and I wanted to have a logical conversation. A lot of guys will begin to answer your question and then start talking about something else.

Doug Sanders, *former PGA Tour player:*

We had a lot in common. He thanked me for the colors I brought to the game, and I told him that I wished I had worn a cap like he did because then I could have added another color. Whatever he put on, he looked good in it. Very few players could have done what he did. You've got to have the personality for those things to fit together, and he certainly did. Without the personality, he never would have even thought about putting those outfits on. You would never see Arnold or Jack or Gary out there in knickers. It's not them.

Greg Stoda, *sports columnist for the* Palm Beach Post:

I used to play basketball on his driveway in Dallas. After the Byron Nelson tournament or the Colonial, several of his college buddies would congregate over there. A pickup game would ensue and people would be drinking beer. This was driveway basketball, nothing formal, yet he never wanted to lose. There were some elbows thrown and when the game got close at the end, it was more fiercely contested than it was planned to be when things had started out.

Steve Szurlej, Golf Digest *photographer:*

I did a shoot at The Woodlands in Houston for a story about him finally getting the monkey off his back. This was when he won the Bay Hill tournament in 1987 after coming in second in so many tournaments. We even hired a chimp for the shoot. I didn't know Payne well at that point, but he took to that chimp like a kid to a puppy dog. He had no hesitation whatsoever. He held it, he touched it, he petted it. A lot of players might have been hesitant to do any of that. Even I was a little bit hesitant. Sure the monkey's trainer was there, but you never knew whether it would scratch or bite you. And Payne gave us all the time we needed.

Of all the years that I worked with him, there was only one time when he bit my head off, and I deserved it.

He was missing the cut at Bay Hill, at his home, which had to be embarrassing. But my office needed a picture of him. So I went to see him, and before I could say a word, he saw me and said, "Now is not a good time." Still, I had a job to do. I started walking with him toward the clubhouse. He finally agreed to pose for the shot and told me to wait for him outside the locker room. But when he got outside, he didn't have his clubs. His caddie had locked them away. When I told him I needed his driver, he really got [ticked] off. "Why didn't you tell me before that you needed the clubs?" He went to the car and came back, but now he was wearing these moccasins with fringe on them instead of his golf shoes. He looked like an Indian. I said, "Payne, where are your shoes?" He looked at me and said, "We're doing it like this or we're not doing it at all." I took the picture. The great thing is, though, when I saw him again a few weeks later, he looked at me and smirked. He didn't have to apologize but I knew he felt bad. I could tell by the look in his face. I appreciated it.

──────

Lee Trevino, *Senior PGA Tour player:*

He always reminded me of the rock band KISS. Those guys went on stage with their faces painted and put on a three-hour concert. Afterward, they went backstage, took a shower, put their regular clothes on, and walked in the streets unnoticed. When Payne went into the locker room or the hotel and put on long pants, a polo shirt, and a sweater, a lot of people didn't recognize him. He had the best of both worlds.

It didn't surprise me that he won two Opens and a PGA Championship. Because when I played with him, I couldn't understand how he could ever get beat. He had the prettiest golf swing, great mannerisms, and a great attitude. I remember opening up a golf course in Missouri at the Ozarks with him and Arnold Palmer. We played a Skins Game. Well, Payne knocked down just about every flagstick. I just kept saying, "Man, I don't understand how you don't win everything out there." But he wasn't fully focused on the game [in those days], and to do well on the PGA Tour, you've got to almost be a loner and practice all the time. I don't think that he wanted to do that. If he had wanted to do that, he could have won three times as many tournaments as he did.

Scott Van Pelt, *Golf Channel reporter:*

He needled everybody constantly. Anytime I walked by, I was going to hear something, whether it was that my hair was falling out or that I wasn't dressed like I should have been. There was always some abuse, and that was fine; I was happy to give it back. But after he had won the Open at Pinehurst, he did an interview with Brian Hammons on our set, so I just hung around outside, waiting for him. He came out holding that trophy like a baby. I shook his hand and just kept smiling and nodding my head. He did the same with me. We didn't say anything to each other for a good long while until finally, I said, "Payne, that's all I've got for you right now." There were no jokes, no abuse. He smiled and said, "That's all I need."

Bob Verdi, *senior writer for* Golf Digest:

I didn't like him for a while, starting with the 1989 PGA. I thought he was exulting in Mike Reid's unraveling, and I didn't think it was very classy, and I wrote that. A while later, Paul Azinger came up to me and said, "I heard you roughed up my buddy." I said, "Paul, did you see that display at Kemper?" He says, "Payne's a good guy, you'll see." And he was right. I think it takes [quite] a man to admit he had some rough edges and try to smooth them out, and that's what he did. He was always a gentleman with me, and I think he knew that, at one point, I had given him a shot.

The greatest testament for somebody usually comes in one's friends, and anybody who touched as many guys in the locker room as he did, and the way he did it, well, I was amazed at the number of players who were devastated. I think Payne Stewart was having a lot more fun than some of the other guys, and the other guys probably knew it and that's one reason they would like to have him around. He would loosen things up in a hurry.

Jack Whitaker, *sportscaster:*

My son was killed in an automobile accident in 1989, and Payne called the next day from Tokyo to express his condolences. Needless to say, I was very touched. The other thing I will always remember is the way he handled the loss at Olympic. He was Nicklausian in defeat. Jack Nicklaus handled defeat and poor luck better than anybody, and that's the way Payne was that afternoon.

—⟨⟨⟨⟩⟩⟩—

Guy Yocom, senior editor for Golf Digest:

The first time I went to see him for an interview, he gave me directions to his house in Orlando. I pulled down to the end of this cul de sac, and he was out there in the front yard, waving to me. I thought it was pretty unusual for a tour player to be waiting like that. I was impressed.

When the conversation got under way, we started to talk about how hard it is to play in cold weather and rain. He's got a great record at Pebble Beach, so he obviously is one player who could manage pretty well in those conditions. We asked if we could take a picture of him in his rain suit. He had no problem. He puts it on, but that was just the beginning. Within no time, we had him down to his long john underwear. He did all this without the least bit of self-consciousness. There are players who won't let you take pictures unless they're thinking about where their logos are. There was one player we wanted to shoot in a surfing outfit, but he complained because he didn't have anything with Tommy Hilfiger on it. To me, that will always be Payne's legacy. He was less self-conscious than any golfer I ever talked to.

The last time I saw him, in March 1999, he gave me directions to his mansion. It was like déjà vu, because I found the place, and there he was, waiting in the driveway again, just like the first time. During the course of the interview, he opened up about a lot of things, such as his ADD, which he hadn't really talked about, and his potential for a drinking problem. He was being openly critical of Ben Crenshaw; this was before he had made the Ryder Cup team. I said, "Payne, you sure you want to say this? Because if you're on the bubble and a potential captain's pick, do you want to get Crenshaw mad at you?" But he didn't care.

He would do anything. He was incredibly cooperative. And he was very kind. One of the other editors in my building was starring in a local play that was set in the early 1900s and needed some plus-fours. He asked me to ask Payne, which I did. He said that it was no problem, brought me upstairs, and took out a giant box of his plus-fours. He said for me to take whatever I needed. If writers ever caught him in a bad moment or in a bad mood, they were liable to get blown off. But if you just kept after him for a little bit, he would break down and the next thing you know, you can't shut him up.

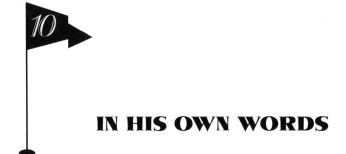

IN HIS OWN WORDS

We all have something in common. We have dreams. The thing about dreams is sometimes you get to live 'em out. And I've always dreamt about playing golf for a living, and here I am living out my dream, and it's pretty special.

—PAYNE STEWART
(1957–1999)

Most times, you couldn't shut him up, which was a good thing. He had a lot to say. Whether weighing in about PGA Tour policy or sharing deeper, more personal reflections, Payne was as candid as any player in the game over the last two decades. Sometimes, too candid. Few players found themselves in as much trouble with either their colleagues or the press. Even just a few days before he died, he was in the middle of another small controversy, this time for an ill-advised impression of a Chinese man, a reaction to a comment made earlier by ABC commentator Peter Alliss. Payne later apologized, and the issue, mercifully, looked like it would go away. Still, whatever the potential consequences, he never changed his approach. Either he couldn't, or he wouldn't. Naturally, writers, even the ones who disliked him, were very grateful. With so many bland players on the tour, they knew they could count on Payne for good copy. They were rarely disappointed.

Following is a sample of comments he made over the years:

———

On failing in his first attempt at the tour's Qualifying School in the fall of 1979:

That's probably the best thing that ever happened to me in golf. I was pretty cocky and thought I was as good as anybody else. When I didn't walk through the Qualifying School like I thought I was going to, I realized I had to work at my game more.[20]

———

On his match against Jim Holtgrieve in the 1979 Missouri Amateur:

I guess I thought I could beat anybody. Jim was the big man in Missouri amateur golf. He had played in the Walker Cup that year. He was Establishment all the way. I was just trying to make a name for myself.[21]

———

On why he quit his job as a stock boy at a clothing store:

I got my check for two weeks' worth—$83. I had just been out on the golf course the day before. I beat some pigeons out of about $150. I went in and quit that day. I went and got my check. I told [his boss], "I appreciate your job, but my job's really out on the golf course."[22]

—————

On the tendency early in his career to falter down the stretch:

I used to be intimidated. If I saw a big name chasing me on the leader board, I'd get excited and tense and stop paying attention to what I should be doing—I'd put some added pressure on myself. I'd tense up instead of just letting my natural ability do it. I'd be forcing things to happen and when you do that, that's when the bad shots creep in.[23]

—————

On his breakthrough victory at the 1982 Magnolia Classic:

God, this is great. It's super. You can't put together a string of victories until you win the first one. Maybe this is the first of many.[24]

—————

On his swing thoughts:

All I think about is the rhythm of my swing. I don't think about my backswing. I don't think about my follow-through. I just think about the tempo and rhythm of my swing. I've been doing it for so long that when I'm swinging in good rhythm, it just comes very naturally to me.[25]

—————

On his decision to wear knickers:

I saw a couple of guys wearing them at a tournament in Asia and they really looked sharp. They kept telling me how comfortable they were, pointing out that on windy days you don't have anything down there flapping around your shoes while you're standing over a putt. That does make sense.[26]

———

On wearing the knickers for the first time in the third round of the 1982 Atlanta Classic:

A perfect debut. We had a huge gallery. The knickers were lavender, and I had nothing but compliments on them. Lee [Trevino, his playing partner] kidded me when he first saw them, of course, but later he told me they really looked sharp.[27]

———

On why he allowed himself to be photographed in a national magazine with a chimpanzee on his back or stripped down to his thermal underwear:

If you can't laugh at yourself, then how can you laugh at anybody else? I think people see the human side of you when you do that. I don't think it's healthy to take yourself too seriously.[28]

———

On losing in the last few holes to Raymond Floyd at the 1986 U.S. Open:

I just got intimidated by the look in Raymond's eyes and didn't tend to my own business. It wasn't Raymond's fault. It was mine. But the Open was right there for me to win.[29]

On blowing the Nabisco Championships, and the money title, to Tom Kite in 1989:

I'll take my $270,000 and go home and cry in my milk, my Anheuser-Busch milk. I'm really disappointed. I got myself in position and let it get away. The more I think about it, the more it hurts. There's a difference between playing safe and playing smart. One of these days, I'll figure that out.[30]

On his behavior—he reportedly yelled an obscenity—after losing the Nabisco tournament to Kite:

I was really mad at the way I had lost, but that just wasn't a professional way to react. I decided I had to change. I just said to myself, "Hey, man, you are thirty-three years old. You've been given a gift. Don't waste it!"[31]

Payne was pretty handy in the kitchen, too. (Photo courtesy of Susan Daniel)

On winning the 1989 PGA Championship:

The way that it was written up was that I got lucky to win the golf tournament because Mike Reid finished poorly. I kind of backed into that one, but, hey, I shot the lowest score for seventy-two holes. Jack Nicklaus won some like that, too.[32]

On winning the 1991 U.S. Open at Hazeltine in an eighteen-hole play-off with Scott Simpson:

This tells me I'm as good as I thought I was going to be. Even when I was young, I always felt I had the ability to win a major championship. My ultimate goal was to win the Grand Slam. I'm halfway there now—I never gave up. It shows me that if I ever do quit, I'm an idiot because funny things happen on the way to the club-house.[33]

—————

On his bunker shot on the last play-off hole of the 1991 Open:

I'm over the shot and I'm hearing a walkie-talkie and a voice, saying, "Get the pin set for the play-off hole, the play-off hole is No. 1." I walked out of the trap and said to myself, "Stand in there and hit this shot and there won't be a play-off hole."[34]

—————

On his attitude in major championships:

This kind of golf really motivates me. Probably one of my biggest problems is I lose focus in some of our PGA Tour events that all kind of blend together. But when I'm at a major, at the U.S. Open, my focus is pretty sharp.[35]

—————

On the pressure he felt as Open champion:

Every time I'd tee off, I'd say to myself, "You're the U.S. Open champion, you're supposed to play well. Everybody's expecting you to play well."[36]

On his slump in 1994 that was partially attributed to a change in equipment:

I have no one but myself to blame for what happened last year. The clubs were not the problem. My brain was the problem. But I've gotten a brain transplant and I'm having a whole lot more fun.[37]

On blowing a four-shot lead to lose the 1998 U.S. Open to Lee Janzen:

I developed a game plan and I stuck to it, and I was very proud of that. I was proud of the way I conducted myself. I was disappointed I didn't win. I didn't play well enough on Sunday to win the golf tournament and Lee Janzen did. He played a wonderful round of golf. I didn't get the job done. It was nobody's fault but my own.[38]

At the 1998 U.S. Open, about how he's learned to handle the media:

I deal with the press better now. I'm not [a jerk] like I used to be. I'm mature. And I understand what the business is all about. You don't have to like it, but you have to accept it. That's one thing my father always taught me. You've got to be able to smile whether you win or lose.[39]

On what kind of Ryder Cup captain he would be:

For sure, I would be a very emotional captain. A very hands-on captain. For example, I wouldn't hesitate to sit somebody down if he wasn't performing, even if he was the number-one player in the world. I've been sat down before.[40]

On his role in the Ryder Cup:

You've got to have people who know how to motivate and to keep people from getting down. I'm that person. I'm a motivator. I get involved. And there's nothing that gives me more pride than being on the Ryder Cup team.[41]

On the possibility of having Tiger Woods as a teammate in the 1999 Ryder Cup:

I haven't been on the same team with Tiger, but I wouldn't be afraid to go up and grab him by his collar and say, "Hey, we're going to win, so suck it up."[42]

On why he conceded the eighteenth hole at Brookline to Colin Montgomerie:

I looked at my caddie and said, "I'm not going to make him putt this putt. My individual statistics don't mean [a thing] out here in the Ryder Cup." I wasn't going to put him through that. It wasn't necessary.[43]

On his feelings for his country:

You know what disgusts me? Every night they play the National Anthem, and I see these professional athletes who are role models—very few put their hand on their heart. Now, I know they listen to it every night, but they don't understand how fortunate they are to live in America. When they raised the flag at my first Ryder Cup, it brought tears to my eyes. I mean, I was representing my country.[44]

On his par putt on eighteen to win the 1999 U.S. Open at Pinehurst:

I can't describe the feeling that was going through my body when I looked up and saw that putt going into the hole.[45]

On his tenacity at Pinehurst:

I kept playing. I kept plugging. I didn't hit the great shots at certain times and then I did hit great shots, and then I'd hit great putts and poor chips, but I got the job done and that means a lot to me.[46]

On fame:

People keep telling me, "You're a star, you're a celebrity." I don't look at myself like that. Because I treat people the way I want them to treat me. I've been successful in golf, and I have some things because of my success. But I don't think I'm better or worse than anybody else. I feel like I'm the same. I mean, God created us all equal.[47]

At an October 1999 dinner in which he was awarded the First Orlando Foundation's Legacy Award:

We all have something in common. We have dreams. The thing about dreams is sometimes you get to live 'em out. And I've always dreamt about playing golf for a living, and here I am living out my dream, and it's pretty special. . . . But really what excites me probably as much as winning is being able to make a difference in people's lives. That's what it's all about. It's not that hard to really give something back.[48]

On playing golf with his father:

He could stick the needle in me deeper than anybody I've ever been around. He'd get me so mad on the golf course, it was scary. And then he knew he had me. I'd end up having to pay him a couple of bucks at the end of the day and that hurt worse than anything.[49]

*Payne loved playing golf with his dad, although Bill Stewart was a
master at knowing how to needle Payne during a round.
(Photo courtesy of Susan Daniel)*

———

After winning the 1999 AT&T Pebble Beach National Pro-Am:

I've grown up. I don't know if I knew what I wanted before.
Now I do. It's my family. I want to see my kids grow up.[50]

———

*Describing his new sense of faith during a press conference after the
1999 U.S. Open:*

I've got to give thanks to the Lord for giving me that ability to believe in myself. Without the peace I have in my heart, I wouldn't be sitting here in front of you right now.[51]

———

On Tracey:

I became more responsible when I married Tracey. I dedicated myself to her and my golf. She is one big reason my game excelled last year. She tells me, "Don't you want to be the best? Why don't you get out there and practice if you want to be the best?" She doesn't let me slack off.[52]

———

On his new perspective:

All of a sudden, golf isn't everything in my life. I have a beautiful family. If, on the way home, something would happen and I can't play golf again, hey, I've had a wonderful career, but I want to be able to spend the rest of my life with my family, and give them all the love that I can. That's one thing that Paul [Azinger] taught me. Golf isn't everything. God's going to call us home sometime. I'm going to a special place when I die but I want to make sure that my life is special while I'm here.[53]

Epilogue

On October 25, 1999, God called Payne Stewart home. He was only forty-two.

Payne was on his way to Texas, first for a meeting on a proposed golf course near Dallas, and then on to Houston to play in the Tour Championship. But the twin-engine Lear jet he was riding in began to veer off course. Air traffic controllers couldn't raise anyone by radio. Government officials believed the plane might have suddenly lost cabin pressure soon after taking off from Orlando. Four hours later, it ran out of fuel and fell to the ground outside Mina, South Dakota. Besides Payne, other casualties included his agent Robert Fraley, the chief executive officer of Leader Enterprises; its president, Van Ardan; architect Bruce Borland; pilot Michael Kling, and copilot Stephanie Bellegarrigue.

Tributes immediately flowed in from all over the country and not just from people prominent in the game. Even President Clinton issued a statement. A few days later, on Thursday morning, as Payne's peers gathered on the first tee of Houston's Champions Golf Club, a lone bagpiper marching through the fog played "Going Home," a song about a Scotsman finally returning to his homeland. "When he died, a big part of us died, too," said Tom Lehman. "He was a very emotional guy. He loved to laugh, and he was not ashamed to cry. I'm not going to be ashamed of my tears this morning, and neither should you."[54] The next day, with tournament play canceled by the tour, Payne's colleagues attended a memorial service at the First Baptist Church in Orlando. Among those eulogizing Payne were his wife, Tracey, best friend Paul Azinger, and longtime swing coach Chuck Cook.

On Sunday, most of the field in Houston donned knickers in Payne's honor. "We're going to miss Payne Stewart," said fellow pro Stuart Appleby. "We're going to miss his passion and his fire. The only thing we'll have is our memories."[55]

END NOTES

1. *www.springfieldmo.org.*
2. *Ibid.*
3. *Q-School Confidential*, by David Gould.
4. *Payne Stewart Memorial Service*, the Golf Channel, October 29, 1999.
5. *Payne Stewart Remembered*, the Golf Channel, October 26, 1999.
6. *Golf* magazine, "Funeral for a Friend," February 2000.
7. *Ibid.*
8. *Payne Stewart Remembered*, the Golf Channel, October 26, 1999.
9. *Ibid.*
10. *Ibid.*

11. *Golf World*, November 5, 1999.
12. CBS coverage of the AT&T Pebble Beach National Pro-Am, February 5, 2000.
13. *Payne Stewart Memorial Service*, the Golf Channel, October 29, 1999.
14. CBS coverage of the AT&T Pebble Beach National Pro-Am, February 5, 2000.
15. *Payne Stewart Memorial Service*, the Golf Channel, October 29, 1999.
16. *Ibid.*
17. *Dodger Talk* on KXTA radio in Los Angeles
18. *Payne Stewart Remembered*, the Golf Channel, October 26, 1999.
19. CBS coverage of the AT&T Pebble Beach National Pro-Am, February 5, 2000.
20. *Golf Digest*, January 1983.
21. *Golf Digest*, July 1987.
22. *Golf Talk Live* on the Golf Channel, September 14, 1998.
23. *Golf Digest*, August 1990.
24. *Golf World*, April 16, 1982.
25. *Golf Talk Live* on the Golf Channel, September 14, 1998.
26. *Golf Digest*, January 1983.
27. *Ibid.*
28. *Golf Digest*, June 1999.
29. *Golf Digest*, July 1987.
30. *Golf World*, November 10, 1989.
31. *New York Times*, May 18, 1990.
32. *Golf Digest*, June 1999.
33. *Golf World*, June 21, 1991.
34. *Ibid.*
35. *Golf World*, June 26, 1998.

36. *San Francisco Chronicle,* June 15, 1992.
37. *Fort Lauderdale Sun-Sentinel,* May 7, 1995.
38. *Golf Talk Live* on the Golf Channel, October 1998.
39. *Golf World,* June 26, 1998.
40. *Golf Digest,* June 1999.
41. *Golf Talk Live* on the Golf Channel, September 14, 1998.
42. The *Scotsman,* March 30, 1999.
43. *Denver Post,* September 27, 1999.
44. *Golf World,* June 11, 1999.
45. *Golf World,* June 25, 1999.
46. *Golf Journal,* July 1999.
47. *Golf Week,* November 6, 1999.
48. *Ibid.*
49. *Golf Talk Live* on the Golf Channel, September 14, 1998.
50. *Golf Week,* February 13, 1999.
51. *Golf Journal,* July 1999.
52. *Golf Digest,* January 1983.
53. *Golf Talk Live* on the Golf Channel, September 14, 1998.
54. PGATOUR.com, October 28, 1999.
55. PGATOUR.com, October 31, 1999.

INDEX

ABOUT THE AUTHOR

Michael Arkush is an associate editor for *Golf World* magazine. He has also worked for the *Los Angeles Times* and *People* magazine. Arkush has written four other books: *Rush!* a *New York Times* best-selling biography of Rush Limbaugh; *Tim Allen Laid Bare*; *60 Years of USC-UCLA Football*, cowritten with Steve Springer; and *Fairways and Dreams*. Arkush lives in Connecticut with his wife, actress Pauletta Walsh, and daughter Jade.